The Love of Roses

From Myth to Modern Culture

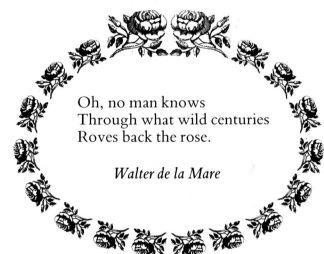

Oh, no man knows
Through what wild centuries
Roves back the rose.

Walter de la Mare

The Love of Roses

From Myth to Modern Culture

Graham Rose and Peter King

Introduction by D.J. Squire

Quiller Press
LONDON

Dedication

This book is dedicated to all those who because of disability
or ill health are prevented from travelling to seek solace in
their favourite rose garden.

Mr D. J. Squire has been associated with the welfare of old
people for over 40 years. A share of the royalties from sales
of this book is therefore being donated to the aged, sick and
terminally ill through the auspices of the hospice movement
and the Abbeyfield Society, which he has been supporting
for many years.

Frontispiece: a detail from *Summer Offering,* painted by
Sir Lawrence Alma-Tadema in 1911, shows his two
daughters holding roses.

First published 1990 by
Quiller Press Ltd.
46 Lillie Rd, London SW6 1TN
Copyright © 1990 Graham Rose and Peter King
ISBN 1 870948 41 6
Designed by Frank Donovan
and produced by Hugh Tempest-Radford, Book Producers
Printed in Italy by New Interlitho

Contents

Contents

Rosa pristina

My life-long love affair with roses began in 1918. Like many children with rural backgrounds, I was given special permission to leave school when I was only twelve, in 1917, so that I could help the war effort by working on the Wiltshire farm where my stepfather was the bailiff. Thousands of able-bodied adults were being killed every day on the Western Front and farmers were finding it increasingly difficult to obtain hands to help with farm work. So I had already gained some physical strength and rudimentary skills as a cultivator when we moved to Essex in 1918, and I was taken on to help with the pack of beagles and act as the garden boy to a Captain and Mrs Paul of Bishop's Stortford in Essex. I was extremely lucky because Mrs Paul was passionate about roses and much of my work entailed moving slowly about after her, collecting the trash as she pruned and dead-headed the rose beds. Although she was in no way intimidating, I held her in great awe because to me her knowledge seemed encyclopaedic. Happily it was something which she seemed compelled to share. She talked incessantly as she worked and I listened hard to everything she said.

Although I didn't realize it at the time, in retrospect it is clear that she was a born teacher, determined to pass on all she knew so that I should become as keen a rosarian as herself. She also knew that a thorough command of all aspects of rose culture would serve as an extremely useful qualification at the outset of a youngster's career in gardening. And I am eternally grateful to her because there is little doubt that the lessons which I learned under her gentle tutelage later proved invaluable to me. For although many of the details may have changed, the principles of good rose growing remain unaltered because there will never be any substitute for good husbandry. And anyone who can master the disciplines required to grow roses properly will have no problem in tending any other sort of woody or herbaceous plant.

Apart from doing the minor chores Mrs Paul taught me how to 'bastard trench' to prepare new rose beds. This entailed removing the soil down to two spade-spits deep, forking the bottom of the trench to improve the drainage and mixing in one barrow-load of slow-feeding, moisture-retaining, well-rotted horse manure per square yard with the lower layer of soil as it was returned to the

PREVIOUS PAGE

Rosa multiflora, a native of China and Japan, is a wild rose renowned not only for its large clusters of flowers but also for its toughness and inclination to ramble. Varieties were brought from Japan to Europe about 1800. It flowers only once each year. It is widely chosen as a rootstock by nurseries because it will adapt to a variety of soils and helps to produce vigorous stems on grafted varieties.

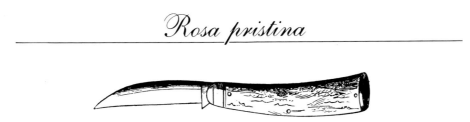

PRUNING KNIFE.

trench. If the roses were to be used as features in mixed beds, I was taught to plant them with their roots well spread in equally well-prepared holes which were one foot square.

Most of the land destined to carry the roses was prepared in the autumn to be ready for the arrival of the new roses from the nurseries. They were usually bunched together, bare-rooted and wrapped in straw and sack. Mrs Paul relied upon my sharp young eyes and dexterous hands to disentangle them from their prickly mass and pick out and cut off cleanly portions of stems or roots which had been damaged when the young plants had been dug out of the ground or during transport: these might act as entry-points for infections.

I was always delighted to do this work because it gave me the opportunity to wield my knife. That was an instrument of which I was inordinately proud because I knew that it distinguished a young professional like me from most amateurs, who used secateurs for such delicate work. But my knife, from which I was inseparable, was sharp as a razor: at least some of my free time every day was spent rubbing it on fine carburundum stone and then honing it on leather, to maintain its ability to guillotine even the most obdurate stem without leaving the whisper of a snag.

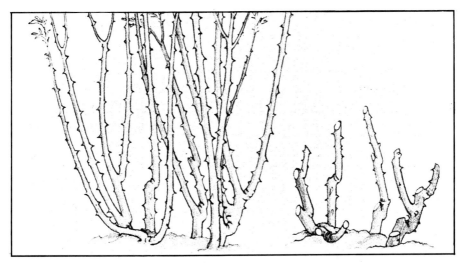

Gertrude Jekyll was one of those who revolutionized the way in which roses are grown in our gardens, calling in her book on roses for them to be displayed against a dark green background, rather than displayed in solitary splendour as was the Victorian preference.

Because Mrs Paul was so strict about seeing that every fragment of perennial weed root was removed when the beds were being prepared for planting, there were few problems. And that was good because deep digging would have been necessary to remove them from an established bed and that would have caused considerable root disturbance which roses hate. That was why she wouldn't allow me to disturb the top soil with a hoe, to remove germinating annual weeds and improve aeration in the spring, until she was satisfied that I would cause no damage. The spring weeding and scuffling was carried out when the likelihood of heavy frosts had passed and just after any plants loosened by the winter gales had been firmly heeled back into place; they had also received their final dormant-season pruning to remove any frost-damaged wood, leaving the bush roses with four or five well-spread strong stems about 5 in. long which terminated in an outward-facing bud. And all this was the prelude to the vital spring mulching.

Mulching was something which Mrs Paul treated with the gravity of a sacred rite and it was a procedure which I later realized was vital, designed to extract the maximum performance from roses, because it fed them, kept the soil above their roots nice and moist during the drier months and helped to suppress weeds.

I can still remember the mixture which we used. And that is no great feat because I still use a modified version of it 72 years later! To every large barrow-load of manure, I had to add 5 lb. sulphate of ammonia, 14 lb. superphosphate of lime, 10 lb. sulphate of potash, 10 lb. Epsom salts, mixing it well before spreading approximately a bushel of it to every square yard of bed surface. Such a thick surface mulch, in which all the mineral ingredients are fairly soluble and quickly available to the plant, can only be of value in the spring and summer when the plants are beginning to grow rapidly and can absorb the available nutrients before they are washed into the drains. So much blanketing organic matter would cause problems if applied at that level in the autumn when it would keep the soil too moist and encourage dankness and the consequent root rots.

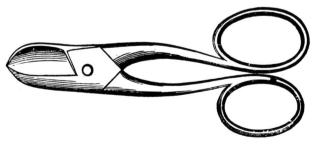

ROSE SCISSORS.

As an autumn dressing, to keep the roses ticking over nicely in the winter and introduce the slow-release organic fertilisers which would provide a reserve of feed when the more soluble minerals had been used up, several good handfuls of a 50 : 50 mixture of blood and bone meal and fish meal were sprinkled over each square yard soil and a good dressing of compost was scuffled into the soil surface.

Apart from a light top dressing in midsummer to help to support the growth of the more vigorous roses, the work which they demanded later in the season was confined to dead-heading, additional light pruning to improve the shape of the plants, trimming away damaged stems, tying up climbers as they developed, and removing suckers from the rootstocks (which was known as 'rogueing'), as soon as they broke through the soil, with a very sharp tool with a V-shaped blade which was called a 'spudder'. Of course, those varieties of rambling rose which only bloom well on wood matured in the previous season had to have next year's flowering stems selected and continually tied-in as they grew; surplus stems had to be pruned away as they emerged.

Precautionary spraying to control pests and diseases before they could do serious damage was the major summer activity in the rose beds. And the products which Mrs Paul considered the most effective were smelly and demanded much effort in preparation. Sulphur and copper preparations were used to control powdery mildew and black spot. Pyrethrum emulsions or derris dusts were used to control most chewing pests, but the biggest chore involved the preparation of Quassia emulsion, for blackfly and greenfly control, which Mrs Paul taught me as though it were a cookery class. I had to take 1 lb. of chips of wood from the *Quassia amara* tree from Surinam and soak them in a gallon water for 12 hours, before melting in ½ lb. of soft soap and bulking it up to 8 gallons of further water before spraying.

All this strange alchemy was used to protect the beauties to which Mrs Paul introduced me. We sprayed them regularly on the splendid yellow climber 'Maréchal Niel', the white Hybrid Tea 'Frau Karl Druschki', the vigorous golden-buff rambler for pergolas and walls 'Emily Gray', the fragrant, flesh-pink rambler 'Dr W. Van Fleet', creamy 'Gloire de Dijon' and – the latest sensation – 'Mermaid', another yellow climber. Mrs Paul was very proud that the British breeders of the same surname (Paul) had brought this out in 1917 as the result of a cross between a double yellow Tea rose and *Rosa bracteata*. All these roses are still favourites of mine.

I took a small step towards becoming a rose grower in my own right in 1927 when, in what spare time I had from my job as second gardener at the naval school in St Margaret's, Twickenham, I helped out during busy seasons on the large Henry Spooner nursery at Hounslow on the site of what is now Heathrow Airport. That is where I learnt the technique of bud grafting which is so essential for the professional rose grower because it enables him to multiply his stock of plants. At its simplest, this involves cutting a bud out from the leaf axil of a recently matured stem and implanting it in a pouch specially prepared for it beneath the skin of a rootstock plant which has already become well rooted in the ground.

Budding was an operation which obliged me to graduate to another type of knife. And when I had learnt to use it really effectively my pride was boundless. A true 'Budder' has to be as scalpel-sharp as any other useful garden knife, but it differs in that the blade is slightly hook-nosed. This enables its body to be held parallel with the stem of the stock when making a shallow longitudinal ½ to ¾ in. cut into its skin with its tip. The hooked shape is easier, too, when making a similar cut at right angles across the top of the first cut, and also when using the blade tip to prise the skin up gently from the harder tissue below to form the pouch to receive the scion bud. Any sharp knife can be used to do this job but the hooked blade makes it much easier. And since I, like every débutant budder before me, found that it was crucifying work, anything that made it easier was more than welcome. Nearly everything happened when you were both crouching and bending far forward. You bent to cut the pouch in the stock. You hadn't time to stretch up before binding the bud into its pouch with a strand of the bass (also known as 'filis') from the hank which hung round your waist – especially if you wanted to keep pace with the real professionals who were known as 'ready bends' because they seemed to do everything permanently bent double. You bent to clip off the projecting tongue of bass by deftly squeezing it between the sharp edge of your budder blade and the pad of your thumb, which served like the anvil of a secateur and which had become so hardened by constant use that it had a consistency resembling that of deer horn! And when you moved on to the next plant you were still bending as you did it, because if the foreman saw you stretching up he would accuse you of malingering. The 'ready bends' even found ways of getting their cigarettes out of their pockets and lighting them without stretching up. All this during working hours which lasted from 7.30 a.m. to 6 p.m., Monday to Friday, and from 7.30 a.m. to midday on Saturday, for a reward which averaged less than £2 per week.

The buds which we used for grafting were cut away from the stems, taking some of the lower tissue with them. After approximately 20 minutes' soaking in water it was possible to separate the

A late nineteenth-century rose garden has recently been recreated in the grounds of Warwick Castle.

skin with its bud from the harder tissue, so that when it had been grafted to the base of the bud it would make direct contact with the cambium of the host stock and be able to be nourished by and quickly become fused with it.

In those days the rootstocks were usually strains of *Rosa canina* which were dug out of the hedgerows by gypsies and offered for sale to rose growers. Those with long and straight stems were used to bud the long-stemmed 'standard' roses. Although these were sometimes somewhat malformed because of the way in which they had grown in the hedgerows when fighting their way up to the light, a feature which gave many of the final grafted 'standards' an

Rosa canina. A wild variety known as the Dog Rose; cultivated varieties are used as rootstocks for budding.

odd shape, they were wonderfully healthy – many roses which were grafted then can be seen still flowering in some of our more cared-for old gardens today. However, it must be said that some of them were rather more mature than was desirable, or their roots had been too damaged when they were harvested, and about 20 per cent of the grafts did not take.

The whole bud-grafting operation was organized on a three-year cycle. There was plenty of chilly work in January and February of Year One in planting out the rootstocks in close lines across the field. In contrast, budding was usually hot work because it took place during June, July and August of the same year. The buds were grafted on to the lower portions of the host's stem, which was otherwise allowed to develop normally in the first year.

It always seemed to be during the nastiest weather in February of Year Two that, with freezing fingers which later developed monumental chilblains, we carried out the 'heading back' and 'rogueing'. The purpose of heading back was to cut away all above-ground portions of the host plant above the bud graft to allow the scion to grow away vigorously, because it then received the full benefit of the sap from the roots. After the summer's growth, the newly budded roses were harvested, trimmed, and prepared for packing and despatch to fulfil orders received earlier in the year. Planted around Christmas when the weather promised to be reasonably clement, in their third year the newly budded roses would be blooming in their new home for the first time.

In 1924, before I became a competent budder, the great Danish rose breeder Svend Poulsen had created the first revolutionary type of rose to appear in my lifetime. By crossing the hardy Polyanthus 'Orleans Rose', with clusters of small pompon flowers, with the Hybrid Tea 'Red Star', he produced the first rose with clusters of large pink, semi-double Hybrid Tea-type blooms, which he christened 'Else Poulsen'. It was the forerunner of a whole new race of roses, first called the Floribundas and now known as Cluster-Flowered roses. As soon as I saw them they seemed to me to be the perfect answer for providing massed colour in a garden. And the wonderful thing is that nowadays they can be obtained as dwarf, medium or tall forms and can meet a great variety of needs.

What I learnt at Spooner's, coupled with a gathering confidence in my abilities as a gardener, slowly enabled my career to progress so that by 1936 I felt confident enough to establish my own garden contracting firm, D. J. Squire and Company Limited, which still trades under that name. Initially, garden establishment and maintenance and turf contracting provided the bulk of the business. But as the firm's prosperity grew, it expanded first into the large-scale production of plants in its own nursery and subsequently, in the 1950s and 1960s, it opened four garden centres in the south-western approaches to London. Throughout the whole period, while broadening the scope of the company's activities, my interest in roses never waned: I followed very closely any developments in their breeding, culture and the ways in which they were being sold.

Overproduction, strong competition and the consequent sharpening of prices, combined with increasingly high postal charges, meant that towards the end of the 1960s sending roses by post or other delivery services was only feasible for firms growing them on a very large scale. Happily this coincided with a rapid

This engraving of a specimen pot rose from a Victorian rose-growers' handbook is typical of the forms common 150 years ago.

growth in the garden centre movement which I can claim to have helped to pioneer in Britain. I was introduced to this novel merchandise during a visit to the USA in 1962 where I saw how well plants growing in old grease and fruit tins were selling on garage forecourts.

The advantage of presenting roses in containers is that the customer can see and take them away when they are in full leaf and flower – and therefore has a much surer idea of their character than can ever be obtained from coloured photographs in a catalogue. The ultimate commercial result of this change was that whereas, prior to 1960, we sold no roses in June and July, these days we sell more than 40,000 in the same period every year.

The popularity of container growing was parallelled by a renaissance in interest in dwarf and miniature roses. A limited range of miniatures was very popular early in the century, but they seemed to fade away after the First World War. More adventurous breeding programmes, coupled with a need for more compact roses to fit into smaller gardens, and the fact that although they hate root disturbances miniatures grow happily in containers and are there-fore ideal for garden centre sales, have led to their revival. The smallest of the miniatures can make good houseplants; probably the best way of handling them is to plunge them into a sheltered spot in the garden until the buds begin to burst and then to take them indoors and stand them on a pebble or charcoal tray which is kept nice and moist, but not so wet that the roots become waterlogged. They need the light of a south-facing window, but ought to be protected from the direct rays of the sun. I always encourage amateurs to multiply their miniature roses by taking 3 in. cuttings above the base joint in the autumn from the current season's growth. If the base of the cuttings is dipped in hormone rooting powder, they will root very well into moist compressed seed compost and soon be ready for potting on.

Over the last twenty years, a much freer attitude towards garden design and a longing for a return to what seemed to be a simpler and more desirable nineteenth-century life, has led to a great revival of interest in shrub roses. First the *rugosa* species became very popular for informal hedging. Then, after David Austin produced his 'Constance Spry' in 1961, rose growing underwent another important revolution as, year after year, he brought out what have been called his "English Roses". With all the charm, fragrance and vigour of the old shrub roses, they have the great advantage of being repeat-flowering.

My opportunity to become a full-scale rose grower occurred when Eric Smith agreed to sell his Halliford rose nursery in 1970.

Eric's father, A. E. Smith, a former employee of the very old-established growers R. Murrell of Roseacre, Shepperton, had started to grow on his own account in 1927 at his Russington Nursery in Shepperton. Ultimately A. E. Smith took over the Murrell nursery and, with his two sons, ran it until they bought the Halliford site in 1950. I only agreed to buy the nursery from Eric, who had lost his brother Raymond and had no-one to succeed him as a grower, if he would carry on with its day-to-day management, because I felt that his experience was invaluable.

Becoming the proprietor of Smith's and being able to offer Squire's roses was a thrilling development for me because both Halliford and Shepperton are so rich in the history of rose growing and breeding. One of the most notable breeders was Henry Bennett, who had changed the whole direction of rose breeding when, in 1882, he crossed 'Devoniensis' with 'Madame Victor Verdier' to produce one of the first of the Hybrid Tea roses, now called Large-Flowered roses. He was an amateur rosarian who used his record keeping and scientific approach as a cattle breeder when hybridizing roses: he could certainly be called one of the fathers of scientific rose breeding. We have now expanded the rose nursery and have 15 acres planted with a large number of varieties. They make a very fine show at the height of their flowering season in June and are an excellent background against which we hold an annual open rose show under the auspices of the Royal National Rose Society.

A typical rose show in the 1930s, held in Southport, with A. E. Smith (centre, wearing spectacles).

Left Gertrude Jekyll believed that the beauty of roses would be greatly enhanced if the rose garden was planned so that dark shrubs and trees bounded it on all sides. Her book included a plan to show this. Around the central rose area was a wide grass walk and beyond that the dark shrubs. She wanted to show off the 'tender colourings' of the roses because, she wrote, a 'Rose garden can never be called gorgeous' and such a term should be reserved to describe the brilliant blooms of other plants.

Right M'Intosh, a Victorian pundit, describes this as a plain geometrical garden which 'upon a small scale' would make a good size garden, 'standard roses being planted in rows parallel with the walks'. The centre elliptical figure would be of dwarf roses. 'Standard roses are much improved,' he adds, 'both in strength and appearance, if their stems be nearly enveloped in moss'.

Each year, as I watch the staff tidying up after what is always a delightful day, I find myself reflecting upon all the changes which have taken place in rose growing since I first learnt the rudiments from Mrs Paul. Apart from the container growing revolution, there has been a fundamental change in the rootstocks employed when bud grafting. Nowadays most 'standards' are budded onto straight stems of *Rosa rugosa* or the 'Pfander' selection of *Rosa canina*. Most of the other forms are budded onto *Rosa coriifolia* var. *froebelii* (formerly known as *Rosa laxa*). These are nearly all imported in their millions from abroad, where the standards of selection are so rigorous that good growers have little difficulty in obtaining an almost 100 per cent 'take' of their bud grafts.

Another great change has been the need to search for substitute forms of organic matter for what used to be the ubiquitous stable manure. Captain and Mrs Paul, like the owners of all large houses, had an ample home supply from their own stables. But even close to the centre of towns, the horse played such an important rôle in the movement of goods and human transport until the late 1920s that stable manure was readily and quite cheaply available to anyone who needed it. Since the motor car replaced the horse, peat has, for the last half century, provided the bulk for mulching or improving the condition of soils. However, with environmentalists dubious about the wisdom of depleting our peat beds, it seems likely that an alternative may have to be sought.

Probably the most important development in recent years has been the micropropagation of roses. This laboratory technique (which is discussed in some detail later in this book) involves growing whole new plants from just a few cells taken from the parent. Its implications are astonishing when it is known that from a single plant it is now possible to obtain thousands of laboratory-produced clones in a single year.

I wonder what Mrs Paul would have thought about that. I expect that after a period of careful thought she would have

The 'Violet Squire' rose, a good example of a modern Hybrid Tea rose, first produced for D. J. Squire's Golden Wedding anniversary, 1970.

approved, because she would have felt that it would help everyone to share her ambition of always having 'a rose looking through my window'. And I have no doubt that she would have greatly enjoyed this book to which, as a professional rose grower, I have been delighted to write this foreword.

As a much older man than the authors, I hope these notes will give some flavour of what gardening in general, and rose growing in particular, was like in the first three-quarters of this century. This book is a welcome change from the many lavishly illustrated books on roses which always seem to me to be little more than superior catalogues. It is certain to appeal to rose lovers because, while it is less concerned with long descriptions of varietal characteristics, it really examines in profound detail all those fascinating aspects of rose culture, utility and myth which have hitherto been ignored.

David Squire
Laleham-on-Thames, 1990

Rosa antiqua

Plants which were undoubtedly roses, recognizable by the general character of their blooms and foliage, were portrayed in murals and sculptural reliefs from the earliest historical times. And the classical literature of both the Orient and the West contains plenty of references to them. However, because artists are notorious for distorting or ignoring details to improve their compositions, and writers are often as concerned with style and effect as they are with fact, we are not quite certain which species of rose early gardeners raised.

These could not be identified with any confidence until orderly Renaissance scholars had equipped themselves with magnifying lenses in order to study plant morphology. Unlike the artist they were imbued with a desire to classify and describe in precise detail. Historians, botanists and geneticists considering the sum of the evidence and the distribution of the simple species roses today have concluded that by the time of the Roman Empire, rose growing had been developed to a fine art.

The simple species, while attractive when in flower, would only have had a very limited flowering period in midsummer and would rarely have flowered again in the autumn. To help to prolong the period when roses were available for special occasions, the Romans are believed to have had roses grown in Egypt and other places in the Middle East, from where they were shipped to Rome while still in bud. The roses which the Roman throngs crushed beneath their feet were likely to have been selections from the naturally occurring variants of the few species thought to have existed in Europe at that time, or hybrids between them. Notable among them could have been *Rosa canina*, *Rosa* x *alba*, *Rosa gallica* and *Rosa damascena*.

Rosa canina, our common hedgerow dog rose, with hostile strongly-hooked thorns on arching branches up to 10 ft. long, and pink-to-white flowers, is very variable in form. More than 60 varieties and forms have been listed. This is probably due to the fact that, as the result of an evolutionary quirk, its chromosome content also varies. In some forms it has 28 chromosomes and in others 35. *Rosa* x *alba*, known as the White Rose of York, is believed to be a cross between *R. canina* and *R. gallica*. It has rather upright stems growing to nearly 7 ft. and white or very pale pink often semi-

PREVIOUS PAGE

The Gallica 'Officinalis', also called the Apothecary Rose, was often made into a fragrant powder in early times and employed for its pharmaceutical properties. Since the Middle Ages it has been grown around the famous French rose centre of Provins and is therefore also known as the 'Provins Rose'. 'Officinalis' is Latin for 'workshop' or, as we would now say, 'laboratory'.

double flowers. *Rosa gallica*, known as the French Rose or the Rose of Provins, only approaches 3 ft. tall and has stems on whose surface thorns and bristles are densely mixed. Its single flowers are mostly deep pink to red in colour. However, they exist in very many forms. Two of the best-known are 'Officinalis' – the Apothecary Rose or the Red Rose of Lancaster which has semi-double crimson flowers with yellow anthers; and 'Versicolor', a highly decorative mutation from 'Officinalis', which is also known as 'Rosa Mundi' and has white, red or pink striped petals.

Rosa damascena, the Damask Rose, bears pink to red double, very fragrant flowers on arching stems up to 7 ft. long. It, too, has a variable chromosome number and has been recorded in many different forms. Alone among the early roses which gardeners in Europe are thought to have cultivated, *Rosa damascena* has some limited capacity to flower again towards the end of the summer.

Other likely contributors of genetic material to the early hybrids were probably *Rosa rubiginosa (Rosa eglanteria)* the Sweet Brier or Eglantine, which is another strong grower with stems capable of reaching 10 ft. and single pinkish flowers; *Rosa pimpinellifolia*, the Burnet or Scotch Rose, a compact shrub with white or pinkish single flowers; and *Rosa moschata*, the Musk Rose, with small white flower clusters with a strong beeswax scent which appear late in the summer and carry through until the first frost.

At one of the finest rose gardens in England, Kiftsgate Court in Gloucestershire, 'Rosa Mundi' are grown in a bed, despite their short flowering season.

An engraving of a rose arbour, dated about 1600, showing a similar structure to that developed by the Egyptians two millennia earlier to ripen vines.

While they could have been most attractive for a short period in the summer, gardens planted only with these species roses would have been very dull places for most of the year, so the concept of the kind of pure rose garden which became popular in the nineteenth century would have had little appeal. Apart from their usefulness, however, their charm when in flower must have made them a mandatory ingredient in any serious garden. Certainly the Romans seem to have developed rose culture into a fine art and to have mastered the techniques of grafting and vegetative reproduction which would have allowed the most impressive naturally occurring new forms and hybrids, many of which are known to have been sterile, to have been quickly multiplied.

The simple roses which were known to the Romans are also likely to have grown early in the tiny garths which were created as gardens high up among the turrets of medieval fortresses, remote from the stink and clamour in the courts below. And we have plenty of visual evidence that, in more peaceful times, they featured in the gardens of manor houses as both useful and ornamental plants, and also even as hostile hedges to prevent the entry of marauding animals. Roses were also certainly known to have been essential plants in the tiny remote 'paradises' created beyond the apse of monastery churches, where the monks could indulge in quiet contemplation. They are also known to have featured in the apothecary gardens which were always located close to the monastery infirmaries.

By the late sixteenth century, the double and highly-fragrant Cabbage or Provence Rose, *Rosa centifolia*, had become available to gardeners. Its one hundred white to dark-red petals resisted bleaching in bright sunlight. A complex hybrid between *Rosa gallica*, *Rosa moschata*, *Rosa canina* and *Rosa damascena*, its origins are obscure. The splendid series of Moss roses which appeared later, *Rosa centifolia* 'Muscosa', with the moss-like hairs wrapping their calyces, are known to have resulted from the Dutch breeders' attempts to improve the Provence roses by including *Rosa phoenicia* (which resembles *Rosa moschata*, but has several yard-long whip-like stems and corymbs of two-inch diameter white flowers). These Centifolias were greatly welcomed by late seventeenth-century and eighteenth-century gardeners, who were able to introduce much greater variety to their gardens.

Although most of these earlier hybrids had a fairly short flowering season and the majority of them were singles, many of those which have survived are extremely pretty. 'Rosa Mundi', for example, is still very popular because it is as chic as anything which a designer could dream up today; it is still being offered in the catalogues of specialists in old roses in Britain like Peter Beales of Norfolk or John Scarman of the Rose du Temps Passé nursery. The charms of 'Rosa Mundi' are too short-lived, however, to tempt most people to grow it *en masse* in a bed and allow it to dominate the planting in a garden. This is why what documentary and pictorial evidence we have suggests that, until the early 1800s, roses were used in the same way that we use spot plants today – located individually in places where they would be sufficiently prominent

Distinguished rose growers who specialize in old-fashioned roses like Peter Beales (left) and John Scarman (right) still offer 'Rosa Mundi' in their catalogues.

Rosa centifolia 'Parvifolia' was known before 1664 and is a miniature rose usually under two feet in height.

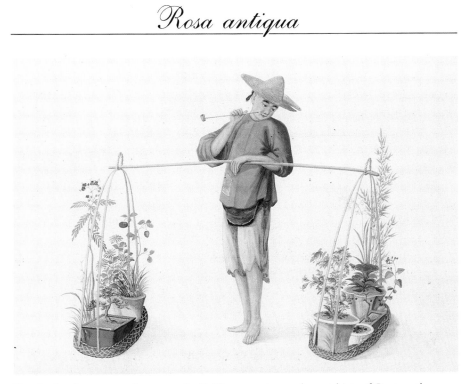

Hundreds of roses grew in pots at the Fa Tee nurseries on the outskirts of Canton: they were carried to European purchasers in these curious baskets. This watercolour from Canton is dated about 1790.

when looking their best, but where their presence would be unobtrusive when their charms began to fade.

The creation of the pure rose garden of the type with which we are familiar today was not possible before the arrival in Europe of the truly recurrent flowering *Rosa chinensis* from China. Apart from the surprise felt by mid-eighteenth-century travellers at the highly developed, if alien, civilization which they encountered when first arriving in Canton, the gardeners amongst them must also have been astonished to find hundreds of roses growing in pots at the Fa Tee nurseries on the outskirts of the town. While obviously recognizable as roses, they were smoother-stemmed and their leaves only had between three and five leaflets, which were a much darker and shinier green than those of the roses commonly encountered in Europe. Their fairly simple double flowers had either white, pink or red petals, but the most remarkable thing about them was that they flowered fairly regularly throughout the summer, with a peak flowering period in the spring and autumn.

Since these roses were frequently pot-grown, travellers – recognizing the value of their repeat-flowering characteristics – had little difficulty in bringing them back to Europe. And their arrival heralded an era of intense rose breeding activity which led to the production of roses of such varied characteristics and abundant capacity to flower over long periods that they made possible the establishment of genuine rose gardens. This was a possibility clearly understood by Empress Joséphine, whose contribution to rose cultivation is described in another chapter.

Joséphine's garden at Malmaison can be considered as one of the world's first genuine rose gardens. Her 'jardin à l'Anglaise' was an innovation in garden design which had paths meandering between bed after bed of roses grown as bushes, or standards in pure stands on bare soil. Sometimes the paths ran beneath rambler-clad pergolas and arches, or between roses on pillars, obelisks or trellis screens, or specially constructed metal frames on which roses were espalliered and made to adopt ornamental shapes like goblets or candelabra. Joséphine created something highly contrived and charming which epitomized a stagey style of gardening that became known as 'gardenesque', and for its management demanded the labour-intensive techniques of high gardening.

As well as the many hybrids of the species roses which had been selected in Europe prior to the 1770s, Joséphine could include a host of new repeat-flowering China roses in her garden. Apart from the lovely clear pink-flowered 'Old Blush China', there will certainly have been the bright scarlet hybrid with *Rosa damascena* 'Duchess of Portland', which her ladyship is said to have found near Paestum, south of Naples, and probably other Portland hybrids.

In 1819, a Paris nurseryman, Louis Noisette, introduced a pink-flowered climber which developed as a seedling from a cross between *Rosa chinensis* and *Rosa moschata*, made in America by an acquaintance of his brother Philippe. This was the first of a series of hybrid recurrent-flowering climbing roses with clusters of flowers which have white, pink or yellow flowers, among which the pure white, double flowered 'Aimée Vibert' is a notable example.

From the island of Bourbon (now named Réunion) in the Indian Ocean came the first roses to bear that name, which were sent to a M. Jacques, gardener to the Duc d'Orléans. They were launched in the trade in 1822 under the name which they had been

Bourbon Rose. This illustration from Krüssmann is after Redouté, where it is named *Rosa canina burboniana*. The rose, descendant of *R. x odorata* and *R. damascena,* originated in the Isle of Bourbon, which is today called Réunion; it was given that name when it was brought to France in 1817.

Rosa hugonis, a yellow-flowering rose, was found in China by Father Hugo, who sent the seeds to Kew in 1899.

given in Réunion, 'Rose Edouard'. One version of the story about their discovery suggests that owners of estates on the island surrounded their gardens with hedges of roses – usually a row of *Rosa chinensis* and a row of *Rosa damascena* – because their matted prickly stems discouraged both people and animals. One estate owner, a Monsieur Perichon, noticed one plant very different from the others and in 1817 a visiting botanist, Monsieur Bréon, realized that it must be a hybrid between the two hedging roses and sent cuttings back to Jacques in France. Another version of the Bourbon story suggests that Bréon was a charlatan with no botanical training, who obtained the rose from a Madame Edouard who had asked a naval officer friend to find an unusual rose for her husband's grave. He is said to have found the repeat-flowering red rose in Calcutta. But whatever their origin it was from 'Rose Edouard' that such rose garden stars as the flesh pink 'Souvenir de la Malmaison' or the white-based, pink-petalled 'Zéphirine Drouhin' were bred.

By 1824 another very significant rose with long light yellow petals and a fragrance of tea, *Rosa gigantea*, had arrived from China, adding clear bright yellow to the hybridizer's palette. Crosses between *Rosa gigantea* and *Rosa chinensis*, both vigorous ramblers,

The early garden at Hatfield House, Hertfordshire has been transformed by the skill of the present Marchioness of Salisbury, and part of it planted with a splendid display of old roses.

provided stocky bushes with blooms with high-centred buds which became known as Tea roses because their aroma reminded people of fresh China tea. The first of these, sent to Sir Abraham Hume by the East India Company from the Fa Tee nursery in Canton, arrived in 1810; since it had pink flowers, it was christened 'Hume's Blush'. The Tea rose hybrid which sold well after its creation in 1851 and still sells well today is the creamy-buff shaded with pink 'Gloire de Dijon'.

With all this genetic raw material available and a more highly-developed knowledge of the sexual reproduction of plants, rose breeders began the hybridizing programmes which have led to the astonishing diversity of form which roses display today. The use of Tea roses in crossing ultimately led to the production of the high-budded Hybrid Teas which, from their first appearance, played such a dominant rôle in rose gardens that the rising middle classes adopted in spirit – if not quite in grandeur – the style created by Joséphine at Malmaison.

During the last century and a half, several other species of roses have had a strong influence on the appearance of our garden roses. Before 1868, *Rosa multiflora* had arrived in Europe from Japan. Its habit of producing a great many small single flowers in clusters was linked in crosses with Hybrid Teas to produce a whole range of dwarf Polyanthus roses, with double flowers in clusters, of which 'Mignonette', with blush pink to white flower clusters on a dwarf bush, is one of the earliest varieties still in production. And it was from the same stock that the later larger-flowered Floribundas like the semi-double 'Pink Parfait' were developed. It was from Japan, too, that *Rosa rugosa* in several forms reached Europe before the end of the eighteenth century. Its vigour and great hardiness, the fact that it will continue to bloom well without being pruned, and the simple fresh attractiveness of those blooms have led to its being used to produce many fine hybrids, with beauties like the magenta pink 'Belle Poitevine', the pristine white 'Blanc Double de Coubert' and the crimson-flowered 'F. J. Grootendorst' among them. Another highly influential rose is *Rosa wichuraiana* from China which arrived in Europe during the 1860s. It has very vigorous stems of 20 ft. or more and dark shiny foliage with a profusion of single white flowers. It contributed a great deal to some of our finest climbers and ramblers, with the lemon-yellow flushed, creamy white, semi-double flowered and still ubiquitous 'Albéric Barbier' and the copper-leaved and pink-bloomed 'Albertine' as prime examples.

By 1891 the strident yellows and orangey reds of *Rosa foetida* – the Austrian Brier, an ill-named native of Iran and Kurdistan – had been transferred to other hybrids, and this added to the palette of colours which breeders had available.

Frequently when breeders wished to miniaturize the blooms of roses, they would use *Rosa pimpinellifolia* in their crossing programmes, in the hope that the charming small flower characteristic of the Burnets would be transferred to the progeny.

By the end of the nineteenth century, nurseries were able to offer bush or standard roses which varied in height between 18 in. and 10 ft. with climbers capable of reaching 25 ft. or more against sheltered walls. Their blooms could vary from tiny white florets borne in clusters to vividly coloured, almost saucer-sized flowers, with a single whorl of petals or crush-petalled Bourbons as big as tennis balls. This huge choice gave designers the opportunity to make rose gardens in which roses of different heights could be arranged in tiers on flat land, or of similar heights planted in steps on sloping land to form 'rose cascades'. To increase the interest of such arrangements, the varieties used could be chosen because their flowering periods arrived at different times, which meant that the colour emphasis of the bed would also change as the season progressed. Apart from being tied onto or trained to attach to rigid structures, climbers and ramblers could be made to spread along swags of stout rope or chain to make a garlanded effect. Man-made rose 'trees' could be formed by intertwining the flexible young stems of ramblers and climbers within a vertical supporting frame and removing any side branches as they appeared to preserve a clean stem up to the desired height. When the twisted stems had aged to become strong and woody, the supporting frame could be removed to leave the self-supporting 'tree'.

In the second half of the nineteenth century, many gardeners seem to have reacted against the craze for carpet-bedding and substituted roses for the annuals in either regular or fancy shaped beds set in stretches of smooth lawn.

Gustav Klimt in his painting *Obstgarten mit Rosen* of 1911 hints at a freer use of roses when he depicts bushes and standards set in a flower meadow beneath orchard trees. And many of today's less formal gardeners seem to be readopting this approach to rose gardening, often favouring the use of old fruit-trees as growing pillar supports for climbing roses – particularly those of extra vigour like *Rosa filipes* 'Kiftsgate'.

With the development of sophisticated rose gardens in which evolved hybrids were planted, the workload increased. The old species roses had required little attention as they were easily propagated by rooting cuttings, or allowed to continue growing on their own roots, and easily pruned merely to tidy them and remove dead wood. But the new hybrids, which were needed in their hundreds if they were to make an acceptable 'show', required a great deal more cosseting. Gardeners, and frequently their employers as well, had to acquire the basic skills of competent rosarians. They had to become familiar with the characteristics of particular hybrids so that they could recognize useful and superfluous wood and understand when and what to prune away to stimulate good growth and flowering in the following season.

Since most of the complex hybrids performed better when grafted onto the roots of vigorous species like *Rosa canina*, growers had to learn to recognize suckers growing from the rootstock and how to amputate them effectively to prevent them from depriving the hybrid stems of energy for growth.

To ensure a sufficient supply of roses of different varieties, to replace losses or fill further beds, gardeners had to become masters of the art of bud grafting which was the most widely adopted form of propagation. This involved removing a bud from some wood on the hybrid plant which had recently flowered, and inserting and binding it ito a specially prepared slit in the bark, low down on the stem of a rootstock plant. When it was obvious that the graft had taken and a new stem had begun to develop from the grafted bud,

From the formality of the earlier gardens, rose growers in the early twentieth century began to turn to a freer use of roses, typified in this painting by Klimt.

all the stem of the rootstock rose above the graft was removed to allow the grafted wood to grow away without any competition. It was a form of nursery garden surgery that required skills of a high order which could only be learnt by much trial and error. Roses being trained as espaliers, or attached to frames, had to have loose stems attached as they grew to avoid them being broken in the wind and their symmetry being lost. Symmetry was considered highly desirable in these rose gardens, whose owners greatly respected all forms of orderliness, and rose gardeners were therefore always vigilant to ensure that neither developing buds, blooms nor foliage were damaged by insect or disease attack.

By the 1890s a good range of fungicides could keep most roses free of blemishes – the duck-egg blue Bordeaux and the wine-red Burgundy mixtures based on copper sulphate protected against downy mildews; sulphur in several forms countered powdery

Rose shows place heavy demands on growers, who resort to such curious practices as this in order to get the best out of their blooms.

mildews; the insecticides included nicotine decoctions, extracts of derris and pyrethrum, and arsenicals like Paris Green or London Purple, used with efficient syringes and knapsack sprayers. There were even metal bonnets which could be attached to branches to protect particular blooms from sun scorch or hail or rain damage, if they were destined for display in vases in the house or for exhibition at fiercely contested rose shows. Since many of these treatments were prophylactic rather than remedial they had to be deployed before the problem appeared, to a tight operational schedule.

Weedkillers were irrelevant in the early days of serious rose gardening because plenty of cheap labour was available. Rose beds were double trenched and every scrap of weed was removed before the roses were planted. From then on, the beds were regularly lightly hoed to prevent the topsoil from consolidating and to eradicate every weed seedling as it developed. Copious watering in dry weather was also considered a vital routine because although roses will stand a considerable drought, they flower much more freely if they are never short of water.

Both water and fertilizer retention was greatly improved, as was the soil structure and its capacity to allow excess water to drain and to enter the root zone. This was the result of heavy mulching with manure, particularly horse manure (many keen rose gardeners also kept horses to pull their carriages), early in the spring. Additional top-dressings of blood and bone meal were also usual.

Rose growers were among the most advanced and competitive members of the gardening fraternity and they readily adopted the latest advances in growing techniques. They were always the earliest to try to benefit by advances made in fertilizer technology. To boost the supply of nutrients to support mid- and late-season blooming, it was always considered good practice to make summer top-dressings with fertilizers with a high potassium content. Wood ash was favoured in the early days, but this was replaced by mineral potash when this began to be mined in Alsace and elsewhere and became available towards the end of the nineteenth century. The salts like potassium nitrate also provided nitrogen to boost plant growth. Better root development was stimulated by applications of superphosphates, which had been developed at Rothamsted before

In Andrew Lawson's garden in Oxfordshire he has planted the rose introduced in 1901 and named after the famous French test gardens Roserie de l'Hay. The rose climbing up the attractive seat is 'Climbing Iceberg'.

1850. Later, advanced synthetic mineral fertilizers like sulphate of ammonia and ammonium nitrate were speedily adopted.

Even people as staid as our Victorian ancestors managed to outdo themselves in the formality of their rose gardens. Many adopted a plan in which five oval lines of roses of increasing height were set inside one another to form a crown of flowers. The planting was completed by eight equally spaced and very tall standard roses set round the crown, like soldiers standing guard round a monarch's catafalque. Few such ambitious arrangements are seen today, but layouts of similar rigidity are still maintained by gardeners using a good blend of modern technology and ancient traditions in specialist rose gardens. These include The Royal National Rose Society grounds, at St Albans in England, Elizabeth Park in Connecticut and The International Rose Test garden at Portland, Oregon (whose director swears by elephant dung, which he obtains free from the nearby zoo), Bagatelle and Roseraie de l'Hay in France, the Sangerhausen Rosarium near Leipzig and the Mainau garden on Lake Constance. Many fine private gardens were made in the 1920s and 1930s. Prosperous members of a growing middle class frequently favoured sunken rose gardens in which the blooms were sheltered from the wind. Their earth-retaining walls, stone steps and paved paths of attractive stone made an interesting foil for foliage and coloured petals. Sadly, too few people can afford to maintain formal rose gardens of that type these days. And provided that they have sufficient room, many modern rose gardeners prefer some of the more recently bred shrub roses which are large and vigorous while still being repeat-flowering.

The advantage of these shrub roses, whether they be the result of recent hybridizing programmes, such as David Austin's New English Roses, or some of the long-established varieties, is that they require very little maintenance. Because they resist disease well, they only need spraying to control bad insect plagues. Their pruning, too, is so rudimentary that it can be very quickly understood and accomplished.

Most rose breeders have responded to the dwindling scale of gardens by concentrating on producing dwarf and even truly miniature roses which occupy much less space. These, plus the more compact bush and standard hybrids, are now frequently being used as feature plants in mixed herbaceous and shrub borders, or in more novel situations such as window boxes, tubs or planters.

Even those purists who formerly would only plant roses in beds of their own have become less rigid in their attitudes. They are prepared to consider planting, at the feet of the roses, spring bulbs followed by massed forget-me-nots. This is in marked contrast to

The Royal National Rose Society grounds at St Albans.

the bleakness of what used to be considered a well-tended rose-bed, which for several months consisted of nothing more interesting than the angry-looking crowns of hard-pruned stems poking through a blanket of rotting horse manure. The latter's aroma was acceptable when gardens were so large that the separate rose garden could be visited only by the professional staff until it was mature enough to be viewed briefly by the owners. But gardens of that grandeur are very rare these days because, even if the space is available, people willing and skilled enough to maintain them are hard to find and very expensive. What used to be a commonplace suburban middle-class hobby has become a rich man's indulgence.

Fortunately the rose is infinitely adaptable. It can be grown in pots, used as ground cover, developed as a hedge, and mingled with other plants in a herbaceous border. The demise of the formal rose garden has not led to any decline in the popularity of the rose as a garden plant, which remains one of the most cherished of garden ornaments in all its various forms.

Rosa romana

III

To put real muscle behind a concept like the beauty of the rose required the power of an empire. The Roman empire

was one of three great empires of its time – along with the Han empire in China, and the Parthian and Sassanian (which reflected the power of Persia) – and their vast domain with a population of 50 million, nearly as big as the Chinese. Although the Greeks had not been intrepid gardeners, they had appreciated the rose and its beauty; when the Romans took over their power base in about the second century BC, they took over the rose too. The conditions of Roman civilization were ideal for roses: great urban centres with huge populations, and an ecomony and infrastructure to match. Water supplies were vital, for transport, for the needs of the citizens and for agriculture. Agriculture was the main source of wealth, and the rose soon became a symbol of that affluence.

Roses were grown commercially and in private gardens, tended by slaves. It seems that the Romans were not satisfied with the single-flowering rose and wanted to extend its season. Virgil in the *Georgics* (Book IV) talks of the festival of Rosalia held on the island of Samos in May and September, which suggests that the repeat-flowering Damask roses were grown there. Paestum, the commercial rose-growing area in the south of Italy, was also believed (probably incorrectly) to cultivate double-flowering roses. And the Romans set up, or encouraged, a rose industry in Egypt: as early as 3000 BC, the rose was sacred to the Egyptian goddess Isis.

The passion with which the Romans embraced the rose was remarkable, quite different in scale from any earlier civilization. It became part of everyday life, their religion, their literature, their festivities and their cuisine.

Krüssmann tells us that the rose was introduced to Rome by Greek settlers. Rhodon was the Greek for rose and Rhodos, which we call Rhodes, was no doubt so-named because roses flourished in its balmy climate and fertile soil. The Rhodians stamped their coins with an image of the rose and called their Spanish colony Rhoda. A river which ran to the sea near Troy was called Rhodios. Greek maps are covered with names which appear to have a rose deriva-

---

PREVIOUS PAGE

Gallica roses were almost certainly grown by the Romans. They were introduced into Northern parts of Europe over the centuries. The origin of this variety 'Cardinal de Richelieu' is not known, but it was probably cultivated in Holland before 1800. By 1870 the previously numerous Gallicas had virtually vanished from the catalogues, superseded by repeat-flowering hybrids.

tion. As early as 446 BC, Herodotus, the Greek historian, describes the roses of Macedonia, growing in the gardens of Midas, as having sixty petals. By the time of Theophrastus (370–286 BC), this has become a hundred-petalled rose which he describes as growing wild on Mount Parnassus, and which was taken from there to be cultivated in Greek gardens.

Theophrastus' book *Inquiry into Plants* gives a detailed description of a number of Greek roses, beginning with the wild rose Dog's Bramble (*R. canina*) which is still called the Dog Rose in English villages today. He also explains how wild roses could be propagated through cuttings or by using suckers. Theophrastus advised, though, that after five years the 'new' bush would lose its vigour and decline. The suggested remedy was to cut it back and set it on fire. Historians tell us that red roses were unknown to Theophrastus – the Greeks only grew pink and white – but if this is so, how did the legend come about that the blood of the scratched Aphrodite turned a white rose into a red one?

The Greeks not only cultivated the rose themselves but also introduced it to Egypt. Ptolemy (323–283 BC), the successor to Alexander the Great after the latter's conquest of Egypt, insisted on growing roses there; the port he created, Ptolemais, is described in Jewish scripture as 'called rose-bearing . . . because of the characteristic of the place'. It is supposed that it was during the rule of the Ptolemies that the Egyptians developed their trade in roses around the Mediterranean. It is thus possible that the Nile was the main source of Rome's earliest rose bushes. Or, of course, they may have developed the rose themselves from the wild.

As early as the third century BC, there was an enormous demand for roses in Rome for making the wreaths and garlands to be awarded to those who excelled in military feats, in sporting challenges and in art. Cato (234–149 BC) encouraged the citizens of

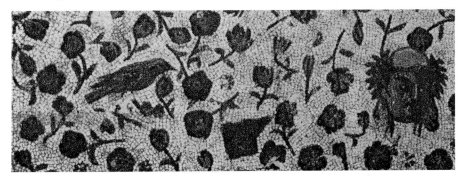

A Roman mosaic with a rose design from the second century AD. It was found in 1903–4 in the ruins of a luxurious Roman villa in El-Djem in the east of Tunisia (formerly known as Thysdrus) and is now in the Museum at Aloui.

Rome to grow roses in their private gardens, while at the same time lamenting that rose chaplets were now awarded for even the most trivial military triumphs, which cheapened their value. The wearing of rose chaplets was forbidden in time of war: the money-lender L. Fulvius, who was unwise enough to be spotted wearing one at the door of his shop during the second Punic War (218–201 BC), was immediately thrown into prison. The American historian Thomas Christopher mentions a rumour that Julius Caesar popularized the wearing of rose chaplets as a means of hiding his baldness, and this might well have been thought to 'cheapen' the chaplet.

This desire to maintain the rose as a symbol of highest achievement is evidence of the kind of status accorded to it by the Romans. Cicero (106–42 BC) condemned the Governor of Sicily, Caius Cornelius, for travelling the countryside under his control seated on a cushion stuffed with rose petals, wearing a wreath of roses on his head, all the while holding a smelling-bag of roses under his nose. Such behaviour would, in our day, be called 'sybaritic'. That word comes from the inhabitants of Sybaris in southern Italy, destroyed by the Greeks in 510 BC, and noted for the gluttony and indolence of its inhabitants. One of them, Sminivides, complained of being unable to sleep because, in his bedroom strewn with rose petals, he had lain on a single folded petal which kept him awake all night. This must be the origin of the Princess and the Pea tale by Hans Christian Andersen.

Excessive use of roses continued to be condemned by Tacitus (AD 55–115) who complained that the Emperor Vitellius, visiting a battlefield after the fray, walked through the unburied piles of corpses only after his route was strewn with laurels and roses. According to Tacitus, the rose was dishonoured and degraded by such actions.

In addition to this negative evidence for the status of the rose, commentators tell us of the part it played in daily life. Krüssmann says that roses were produced for festivals and worn by the guests at important ceremonials. Everyone of status used rose-scented unguents in his daily toilet. Soldiers going on active duty adorned themselves and their chariots with roses. Generals were permitted to bear a rose on their shields, a custom which continued long after the fall of the Roman Empire. Religious ceremonies were not complete without the rose. Streets were strewn with blooms, monuments to the gods crowned with garlands and wreaths. These were made not only of complete flowers but also of individual petals. Those who were wealthy enough to do so reclined indolently on rose petals when they dined, according to Cicero, who criticized the practice.

It is roses, roses all the way in Poussin's version of Arcadia. The painter (1594–1665) is here illustrating a Bacchanalian revel with a full-frontal Pan looking on in apparent approval, yet the revellers are not in a Dionysiac frenzy and certainly not in a Roman orgy.

Roses decorated tombs and were used at funeral services. Sizeable bequests were made to children on condition that they planted a rose tree on the anniversary of the death of their parents. A soldier set aside money in order to plant roses yearly in commemoration of his safe return from a campaign – also perhaps in memory of fallen comrades.

At the great orgies which typified Roman life (at least according to Hollywood), the revellers wore chaplets on their heads, believing it would keep their heads cool and themselves sober. Martial wrote about this:

> In thy dark wine-cup mingle summer shows
> And wreathe thy temples with the blushing rose.

The scent overcame the unpleasant stale smell of wine in the hair, which presumably had found its way there because the drinker had difficulty in locating his mouth. Later it became customary to float rose petals in the wine.

Rose-water, in daily use, was on special feast days also diverted to the public fountains. In the Roman kitchens, rose petals were the ingredients for jellies, honey and wine. The young men, inevitably were convinced of the aphrodisiac qualities of the rose and presented spring blooms to their 'mea rosa'. Shops were dedicated to the sale of roses and villagers brought basketfuls to the cities for customers to buy. Garland weavers and garland sellers (coronate and corollarie) found high wages in the cities.

Roses are everywhere in this painting of the festival of Cerealia in a Roman street, entitled *Spring* by Alma-Tadema. One of his most famous works, it is said to have inspired the great epic film-makers like Cecil B. De Mille who used the concept in *Cleopatra* (1934) and *The Ten Commandments* (1956). The painting is dated 1894.

According to rose buffs, the high point of this rose mania (not a term they use themselves) came in the time of Nero (AD 37–68) who, at a single famous banquet, spent four million sesterces on roses and, on another occasion, had a beach strewn with roses before he would walk on it. Krüssmann tells us that one of his favourite techniques was 'to produce at his banquets and orgies a rain of roses falling from the ceiling upon his guests and, on occasion, in such vast quantities that some of the guests were stifled under the weight of petals.'

It has proved difficult to verify this assertion. The latest biography of Nero, which covers his extravagances in some detail, does not mention roses at all. Suetonius, in *The Lives of the Caesars* (Book VI), has something to say about the Golden House which Nero began to build (or rebuild) after the Great Fire of AD 64. The reference, as translated by Loeb, is as follows:

> There were dining rooms with fretted ceilings of ivory, whose panels would turn and shower down flowers and were fitted with pipes for sprinkling the guests with perfumes. The main banquet hall was circular and constantly revolved day and night like the heavens [commentaries suggest it was only the ceiling which revolved].

Note that there is no mention of roses, although perhaps 'flowers' can be taken to include them. Nero was an unpleasant fellow, almost as unpleasant as they come, murdering his mother, his wife, his second wife's son and numerous lesser mortals. In mitigation, it must be taken into account that he had an inferiority complex and that he had a great feeling for art in all its manifestations. As he was about to commit suicide to avoid execution, he is said to have cried out several times, 'What an artist dies with me!' There is therefore nothing inherently improbably about the stories about his excesses with roses, as he certainly believed that nothing succeeded like excess. After all he arranged for Poppaea, one of his wives (who included several men) to be provided with the milk of 500 asses for the daily bath that preserved her complexion.

If hard evidence for Nero's rose mania is difficult to find, the subject may be approached by investigating the physical source for the large number of blooms which such conspicuous consumption must have demanded. Paestum, south of Naples, had apparently been active as a profitable rose-growing area since 600 BC. Roses flourished in its sunny climate and its rich soil. By the time of Augustus it was also fashionable to take a holiday in Paestum to see the roses in bloom. Originally founded by the Greeks, it had been taken over by the Romans in 270 BC. Another commercial rose-growing area (the Romans called these *roseta* to distinguish them from *rosaria* which were private gardens) was the Praeneste, today called Palestrina, about 20 miles south-east of Rome, where the late-flowering *Rosa gallica* was cultivated. A third centre, 30 miles north of Naples, was in the vicinity of Leporia and produced the roses of Campania.

Writers who suggest that the famous rose plants of Paestum flowered twice in the season have been criticized as inaccurate. Here is the comment by N. Young, published in *The Rose*, number 15.

> Probably the oldest and best-established of these ghost roses is the Rose of Paestum, that perpetual flowering rose which, we are so often told, flourished in classical times, and was mentioned by Virgil. It was not mentioned by Virgil. The sole justification for this claim lies in three words, in which the poet makes a passing reference to *biferi rosaria Paesti* – 'the rose-gardens of twice-bearing Paestum'. The epithet 'twice-bearing' (which is not attached to any particular rose, be it noted, or even to the rose gardens, but to the city of Paestum) is obviously ambiguous; it might mean twice in time or twice in quantity. But some five hundred years later, an obscure scholar named Servius, who took it upon himself to edit the works of Virgil, set against this passage the gloss: 'Paestum, a City of Calabria where roses blow twice in a year'. From this point the myth-makers never looked back. . . . Paestum was a famous and flourishing centre of the rose trade, and the 'roses of Paestum' meant no more than we should mean today by the 'cabbages of Covent Garden'. Paestum was the best-known source of roses, but it produced no special variety of its own, perpetual or once-flowering. In describing the town as 'twice-bearing' Virgil probably meant no more than 'fruitful' or 'prolific'. Nevertheless, it is always possible that his 'twice' was meant to refer to time rather than quantity, and that his commentator Servius spoke nothing but the truth. The Romans – as we also learn from Pliny – were familiar with methods of forcing roses by heat, and in an important entrepôt like Paestum there would have been two rose harvests, one forced and one natural. It would therefore have been quite correct to say that in Paestum 'roses blow twice in a year' – only it was not the same roses which flowered both early and late.

It is believed now that the 'Rose of Paestum' was a form of *Rosa damascena* and attempts have been made to persuade the present authorities at what remains of this temple-strewn site to replace the modern roses planted there with this ancient species. Some scholars note, however, that *R. damascena* does not grow wild in southern Italy, and that writers of the Renaissance period describe it as a novelty, recently arrived from the East. If this was accurate, how could it have flourished in Italy a thousand years before?

The American rose historian, Thomas Christopher, says that while the botanical identity of the roses grown at Paestum may have been lost, 'archaeological excavations have exhumed some very pertinent evidence at Pompeii. In the villa called 'House of Venus Marina', a rose painted on the wall by a Roman (anxious to make his courtyard look more rural than it was) has flowers that are small, as ruddy as any Gallica I've seen, and their form is the same: compact, regular rosettes'. In the 'House of the Fruit Orchard', there are painted roses which, to a modern eye, 'don't look like garden roses at all' and are more like wild roses.

If Roman roses could not be persuaded to bloom twice, they could be encouraged to extend their growing season, thus providing petals all round the year. Special glasshouses were built using panes of talc, a translucent stone, with warm water to bring on the blooms. Roses grown in the open were brought on early by digging trenches between the rows of plants, or around them, and filling them with warm water twice a day.

Roman writers on agriculture, such as Varro (117–28 BC) and Lucius Junius Moderator Columella (a hundred years later), describe the method of cultivation as being to prune the bushes each year before the beginning of March, but not, we may presume, down to ground level. A later writer, Palladius, says that the ground around established plants should be well hoed and any weak or defective stems cut away. Cuttings should be set out in November or in the spring, or seed sown in spring, choosing a sunny position. Plenty of manure should be supplied.

Despite all this good advice, demand for roses still exceeded supply and presumably some types of roses were more in demand than others. Pliny the Elder, in his 37-volume *Natural History* which circulated before and after his death in AD 79, describes the plants of his day.

At the height of the rose cult it seems certain that Roman production had to be supplemented by supplies from Africa. The Nile delta and the area around Carthage were favourite sources. Shiploads of cut roses were sent to Italy, a journey of six days, though how the blooms were kept fresh over this period is unknown. One theory is that they were grown and shipped in tubs, but no-one knows. Whether the Egyptian ruling classes also developed rose mania is uncertain, although it is recorded that when

This painting by Alma-Tadema shows the Emperor Caracalla and his wife Greta at the Colosseum. He calculated some 2500 spectators would be visible beneath the roses and painted in every one of them. The artist painted over 300 pictures from antiquity.

Cleopatra (69–30 BC) went to meet her lover Mark Antony in 42 BC, the hall in which the state banquet was held was covered to a depth of two feet in roses. Other sources say it was the throne room which was 'knee-deep' in roses, for which Cleopatra paid in gold. Such reverence for the rose meant a comparative eclipse for what had till then been the Egyptians' favoured flower, the lotus. Incidentally, Chaucer in his poem on Cleopatra describes her as 'Faire as is the rose in May'.

Pliny reports that the Egyptians produced artificial roses, too, cut out of very thin wood-shavings, and coloured and scented with rose balm. As for the origin of the 'real' roses, these, as has been noted, are believed to have been Greek, although at least one of them, the so-called 'Holy Rose' probably originated in Asia Minor. In 1888 the British archaeologist Sir Flinders Petrie, excavating Egyptian tombs dating from about AD 26, found a wreath of roses in good condition which he sent for identification both to Kew and to one of the great rose experts of the day, M. Crépin of Brussels.

He identified it as *Rosa sancta* (= *R. richardii* Rehd), a close relative of *Rosa gallica*, with simple, pale pink blooms, which is not indigenous to Egypt. Thomas Christopher gives a rather different version of this story. He writes:

> In the dry desert air, the wreath's petals had shrivelled, but they still kept their colour, and when placed in warm water, the blossoms seemed to come back to life. Buds swelled, and the pink petals spread, unfolding to reveal the knot of golden threads at the centre just as they must have been on the morning of the funeral. A botanist at Cambridge had little trouble in identifying Petrie's flowers as roses, specimens of *Rosa richardii*, a species already known as 'the Holy Rose of Abyssinia' because at that time it was still a fixture of the Coptic Christian churchyards in that country.

Other such roses were found in graves in Middle Egypt, where there were also frescoes and pieces of fabric, generally with representations of single blooms with five petals, similar to those grown by the Greeks. The 'Holy Rose' (*R. richardii*) still grows in Egypt today, although not in large quantities, and in 1920 a monk reported finding one growing at 8000 ft. in a mountain village in

Alma-Tadema's first painting of *The Baths of Caracalla* was described by a contemporary critic in 1899 as 'wonderful in its classical faithfulness and truth to archaeological detail'. Later the same year he produced this *Caracalla* showing the Emperor entering the baths on a carpet of roses.

Northern Ethiopia, an area where they had formerly grown in abundance around churches.

As time went by, the production of roses in Rome increased to such an extent that dependence on Egyptian supplies waned. Martial the poet (AD 43–104) wrote:

> O Nile, the Roman Roses are now much finer than thine!
> Your Roses we need no longer but send us your corn.

He tells of a ship which brought roses and gifts from Memphis in the Nile delta for the Emperor Domitian, and how disconcerted the Egyptians were to find roses blooming everywhere in Rome. The city at this time (AD 51–96) is described by its inhabitants as a fragrant sea of roses. This did not spell the end of the rose cultivation in Egypt however. Dr Girardi, leader of the scientific mission which followed Napoleon's invasion of Egypt in 1800, recorded that there were still some 500–750 acres in area devoted to rose growing, and that this contained some 30 ovens for the

Cleopatra – here painted by Alma-Tadema – used roses to attract Antony, according to myth. The title of the picture implies that this was their first meeting and the roses may have signified power, being Cleopatra's acknowledgement of Antony's status as Roman leader.

The Victorian vision of Roman life was based on their study of the classics and the paintings by the popular Sir Lawrence Alma-Tadema. Heliogabalus reached the heights of hedonism when he had rose petals scattered so deep on the floor of his banqueting chamber that some of the guests were reported suffocated.

distillation of rose-water for the wealthier members of local society. By degrees, however, the commercial rose area was replanted with cotton, a crop in even greater demand.

To return to Imperial Rome, the picture that remains with us, however difficult it may be to document, is of a population whose upper classes had a frenzied love affair with the rose. A cursory perusal of the Odes of Horace (65–8 BC) sets the tone:

> 'What slender youth, with wealth of roses sheen,
> And with sweet essences besprent, pursues thee?'

> 'Spare not the roses wreaths to twine;'

> 'Scenting our grizzled hair with rose'

> 'The stingy hand at feasts I hate!
> Fling roses!'

Elsewhere, Horace writes of making love in a cave on a bed of roses. For those with more conventional tastes, E.C. Lovatelli, writing in *Die Rose im Alterthum* says that newly-weds and lovers slept on beds strewn with roses, bridal wreaths were made of roses, and lovers hung rose wreaths on the doors of the room where their beloved slept.

Evidence for the kind of roses which the Romans liked is also found in the ruins of Pompeii, destroyed by volcanic eruption in AD 79. There are compact, regular rosettes painted on the walls of the House of Venus Marina and more still in the House of the Fruit Orchard, as well as compact, semi-double blossoms which look like wild ones. In another house, a ceiling panel was found, covering the roses, also pink and rosette-like. Historians deduce from this that the ancient Romans could not have too many roses, even if they were somewhat lacking in variety.

The image is always one of excess. The high-point of the cult comes with Heliogabalus who became emperor at the age of fourteen and was determined to mark the start of his reign with a special feast. He arranged for three showers of rose petals to fall from the ceiling, which they did with such speed and plentitude that several guests suffocated. The emperor had earlier ordered the doors to be bolted and barred; while he sat at an upper level with a few chosen guests, his guests had no means of escape. An image like this was too fascinating to be ignored by the Victorian 'classical' painters: Alma-Tadema's *Roses of Heliogabalus* of 1888 was one of the most popular pictures of the period.

It might be said that the Roman lust for roses was passed on, after some centuries of neglect and misunderstanding, to the Victorians, who, in more pious mood, took it up with great extravagance, although they could never equal the Romans, to whom Elysium itself was, according to Pindar, 'reddening with the rose, their Paradise' or, according to Tibullus, bursting its fields with 'the blossoms of the fragrant rose'. Note the word 'fragrant'. Thomas Christopher believes that the Romans made odour the primary criterion of a blossom's excellence, 'setting a style that lasted two millenia. Only with the introduction of the modern ever-blooming rose did the primacy of perfume lapse' in favour of regularity of bloom and size and colour. Of the roses listed by Pliny, three of the breeds were without fragrance: he suggested that this deficiency made them unworthy of the name rose. It is fortunate for many of our modern breeders that they are not reliant on the ancient Roman market.

Rosa $\overline{IV}$ **sacra**

The rose, so revered by the Romans, was at first rejected by the early Fathers of the Christian Church, suspicious of anything with pagan connotations. However, not only did the rose have too powerful a hold on the general imagination to be ignored, but it came to have a specific and strong meaning for the later Christians, as the medieval church developed its own roseate symbolisms.

It is not clear exactly why the rose was adopted by the early Christians. In her book *Medieval English Gardens*, Teresa McLean states that it was the very asceticism of the church leaders, dogmatically arguing with each other about the basis of their faith, that eventually gave birth to the cult of Mary, the Mother of God, with the rose as her symbol. The desert Fathers of the fourth and fifth centuries after Christ, and the early monastic communities that took some of their dogma from them, 'found the femininity and comfort they needed to sustain them [in] devotion to Mary'. The author believes that the rose had freed itself of initial Christian disapproval by its own irresistibility and had become, even before the Mary cult, a decorative and mystical symbol. Tertullianus, the early Church Father, envisaged Heaven as a place full of singing rose bushes. The story is told of St Francis of Assisi who transformed into roses a bed of thorns which St Benedict had planted to use for the mortification of his flesh. Other saints connected with gardening in general include St Gertrude and St Dorothy, patrons of gardening in Germany, the latter's emblem being a coronet of roses, or a bunch of roses held in her hand. Teresa McLean says that 'Paulinus of Nola (345–431) and St Jerome (342–420) revoked their ban on roses and encouraged the faithful to decorate their churches with them. St Basil (329–79) and St Ambrose (340–97) declared the rose the most perfect of flowers – one which had been without thorns when it grew in paradise, until the disobedience of Adam and Eve gave sharp spikes to its beauty.'

Mary's motherhood was declared a doctrine, and McLean says that 'according to the Christian poets, Mary's motherhood enclosed the whole of heaven and earth within her womb, within the space of a single round rose. The all-in-one, one-in-all rose of love, once praised in pagan poems, became a Christian rose.' She says that the early Church Fathers also began to make the obvious allegorical identification of Mary's inviolate womb with the sealed garden, penetrated only by God.

PREVIOUS PAGE

While the rose has always had sacred connotations, it has succeeded at the same time in invoking profane ones. The old Alba 'Maiden's Blush' is a *Rosa incanata,* named after its fleshy tones, which the less prurient French call 'Cuisse de Nymphe' (*cuisse* meaning thigh).

The rose was not only a symbol, but, says McLean, when red in colour, the symbol of the blood of a martyr. Since the greatest martyr of them all was Jesus Christ, he had a double association with the rose: as the child and creator of the Marian rose and as the supreme rose of martyrdom, with the five petals representing his five wounds. According to Paulinus of Nola, Christ was the 'sun of justice, fount of all good, flower of God' and his five bleeding wounds were the five petals of the red rose; his crown of thorns was the rose bush.

McLean says that it was the doctrine of the Virgin birth that 'expanded Mary's rose symbolism into the most important, com-

St Dorothy, the patron saint of gardening, martyred in AD 304, sent her pagan oppressor roses, although it was winter and none except hers was in bloom. In this fifteenth-century coloured woodcut she graciously accepts a basket of roses from the Christ Child and hands some back for delivery to the brutal Theophilus.

Piero della Francesca, the Tuscan painter (*c.* 1420–92), makes free use of white
and red roses in the background to his Madonna and Child, as both mother
and son had symbolic connections with the plant.

plex and elaborate motif of medieval art and literature, both sacred and profane'. It was not long, she says, before Mary began to be hailed as the Flower of Flowers, and she figured in the stories of saints' lives, especially those in which she intervened directly to help her faithful devotees, in the form of a miraculous appearance of roses. For example, there is a medieval legend which claims that the first roses miraculously appeared at Bethlehem to prove the innocence of the 'fayre Mayden' who had been wrongly accused (we are not told of what) and sentenced to be burnt at the stake. 'She entered the fire, and immediately the fire was extinguished, and the faggots that were burning became red Rose bushes full of Roses, and those that remained unkindled became white Rose bushes; and these were the first Rose trees and Roses, both white and red, that ever any man saw.'

Rose legends reached the height of their popularity in the twelfth century. One of the most famous quoted by McLean is of Josbert, a monk who recited daily the five psalms that begin with the letters of the name Maria.

> On the feast of St Andrew, 1156, the Prior noticed that Josbert was not in chapel with the rest of the community at prayer time. He went to look for him in his cell, and found him dead, with a rose in his mouth, one in each ear and one in each eye: one for each of the five letters of the name Maria. This little story has all the favourite ingredients of twelfth-century religious symbolism: monastic devotion to Mary; her intimate rosy reciprocity; the sacred number five, reminiscent of the five wounds of Christ, and the rose as a token of love for the departed.

This early German painting *The Virgin with a Rose Branch*, School of Schongauer, illustrates the powerful symbolism of the rose to which Mary directs the attention of the faithful. It was only later, in the sixteenth century, that the word rosary came into common use.

If Josbert's roses were not placed in position by miraculous forces, how did they get there? Monastic gardens and burial grounds are often planted as rose gardens in prefiguration of the Paradise garden, and as a symbol of Mary (indeed, English rose gardens came to be called Mary gardens); thus a friendly brother monk might well have adorned his corpse so that the devout Josbert could continue to love Mary in death as he had in life. It may be noted that Josbert did not have a rosary or string of beads in his hands. This may be because, according to the *Oxford English Dictionary*, such beads did not come into common use until the sixteenth century. The Rosary as a form of prayer or set of devotions consisted of the recitation of a large number of *Aves*, every ten of them preceded by a *Paternoster* and followed by a *Gloria*. Such a large number of devotions needed a set of beads to assist in the memorizing of them, but the beads most commonly in use constitute a chaplet or a third of a Rosary, which provide for five *Our Fathers* and five decades of

A fifteenth-century German woodcut of the Madonna with the Rosary. Mary is enthroned as the Queen of Heaven with figures representing lay and clerical life on either side. The ten circles, interspersed with roses, represent the five sorrowful mysteries of the Virgin (white borders) and the five joyful mysteries (pink borders). Ideally a rosary should have represented fifteen mysteries.

The 42 ft. diameter rose window at Notre Dame (1163–1235), one of the oldest French Gothic cathedrals, is compared with the rather more delicate window at St Ouen, Rouen (1318–1515). These are also sometimes described as wheel windows.

Hail Marys after each of which usually follow five *Glory Be to the Fathers*. The use of the number five thus preceded the invention of the beaded rosary, but the name may have something to do with the number of petals on the flower.

McLean says that wreaths, crowns and garlands were hung on church statues of the martyrs and of the Virgin in her month of May, 'just as they had been hung in Greek and Roman temples'. The medieval cult of the Virgin Mary brought the virginal and the triumphant together in this one symbol (the garland), the age-old defence of the closed circle against evil, the symbol of perfection, virginity and victory (over death) and completed its Marian dedication by making that symbolic crown out of roses.

The shape of the rose was adopted by the priests and lay brothers who built the earliest churches and cathedrals and found its most celebrated forms in the rose windows in stained glass. The psychologist Jung describes these as the most splendid examples of abstract mandelas (magic circles). He says: 'These are representations of the Self of man transformed on to the cosmic plane (a cosmic mandela in the shape of a shining white rose was revealed to Dante in a vision).' More prosaically, it has to be admitted that the origin of the rose window is unclear. Found in early Gothic cathedrals in France, there is a tradition that (like the rose itself) the

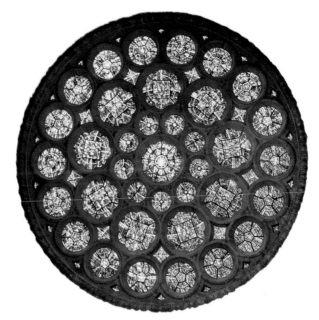

This modern rose window at St Albans Cathedral replaced one which had been plain glass since the nineteenth century: it is said to be one of the largest in the United Kingdom. It is 30 ft. in diameter and was designed by Alan Younger.

design was brought there by crusaders returning from the Middle East. One possible model is the Mosque of Ibn Touloun in Cairo, whose windows of cusped circles are not unlike those in the cathedrals. In England, the rose window at York is one of the most famous, and on the Chapter House in York Minster is a Latin inscription which, translated, reads, 'As the rose is the flower of flowers, this is the house of all houses.'

Several legends are associated with the thousand-year-old rose tree which grows against the walls of the abbey at Hildesheim in Germany. One of these recounts how the Emperor Ludwig, hunting wild boar in the area, had to spend the night in the forest. For protection he built an altar of sorts by hanging his chain and gold crucifix on a thorn bush. His retinue found him – unharmed – the following morning, but the thorn bush had changed into a rosebush. Ludwig ordered a chapel to be built alongside it, which was eventually developed into the abbey and cathedral. It is unlikely that the rose is in fact 1000 years old.

As Christianity became more powerful, the rose quite lost, or absorbed into itself, its pagan symbolism. By the Middle Ages, Venus, once a supreme rose image, had become identified with the medieval sin of *luxuria* (sensuality) and a symbol of the idle dalliance to be overcome by Chastity. According to the *Penguin Who's Who in the Ancient World*, 'Venus was the focus for all the medieval fear of nudity and paganism.' For the time being, Mary had triumphed. Marina Warner, the historian of Marianism, says that 'Mariological mysticism lay in bud until the 12th century when it opened its full glory in the impassioned love and language of St Bernard . . . [who] gave 86 sermons on the Song of Songs.' The latter gave particular poetic emphasis to the lily which shared a religious significance with the rose, no doubt because in pagan times it had been a symbol of fertility. The rose itself is not mentioned in the Bible, although the word was used in error by translators.

McLean says that the significance of the lily arose because the 'early identification of Mary with a red and a white rose . . . was never a poetic success because there was no such rose, and the image was too artificial; the double image of the rose and the lily was much more popular'. The rose that survived was, therefore, the red, or purple, rose. The Romans had described their roses as purple

The rose tree at Hildesheim Cathedral, Germany, is said to be 1000 years old. This drawing by J.L. Brands was published in 1825, but is said to be inaccurate in almost every respect.

and the adjective 'rosy' became synonymous in late ancient poetry with purple. McLean describes how this was taken up by the medieval poets, quoting a fifteenth-century carol to the Blessed Virgin:

> the purple rose
> That whylom [once] grew in Jericho

One of the earliest botanists, Ishak–Amrâm, who practised in the ninth century AD, speaks only of the two species of cultivated roses, white and red. It is true that, by the eleventh century, other colours are being recorded, including 'la blanche nuancée de rouge', but it is the red and white which predominate in literature and art. And it is the red which becomes the specific mark of the Marian rose. Both

VENUS.

An unusual *Venus* but, like the Roman goddess, well-acquainted with roses. Beardsley produced this in 1895 as a frontispiece for *Venus and Tannhäuser*, but it was not used. Venus had acquired sensual symbolism by the Middle Ages.

red and white may have been found in nature, but the red is the rose of myth, legend and, indeed, the essence of the rose itself.

Why is this? Undoubtedly the adoption of the red rose as the symbol of the blood of martyrs and of the Christian virtues played the predominant part. *The Golden Legend*, Jacobus de Voragine's thirteenth-century lives of the saints, says that St Cecilia wore a crown of roses given her by an angel as a tribute to her virtue. St Dorothy is said to have sent a basket of heavenly roses down to her earthly executioner. Another reference to Mary explains how, when she was laid in her sepulchre, 'she was environed with flowers of the roses that was the company of martyrs'.

Religious symbolism continues to hymn the rose in general, as in Dante's *Divine Comedy*, in Paradiso 23, where Beatrice asks

> Why does my face enamour so, that thou
> On this fair garden has no glance bestowed
> Which flowers beneath Christ's rays?
> Behold it now!
> Here is the Rose [la rosa] wherein the Word of God
> Made itself flesh.

Other examples include the English poet Christopher Smart's verse 'Bless Jesus Christ with the Rose', and the many paintings of the Virgin, some of which are illustrated here. Throughout, it is the red rose that has taken over from the white.

As noted elsewhere, the rose had significance in other religions besides Christianity. Vishnu formed his bride Lakshmi from 108 large and 1008 small rose petals. The Persians recorded that once upon a time the flowers complained that their queen, the lotus blossom, slept by night. In order to bring about a reconciliation, Allah named the white rose Queen of Flowers and the nightingale, a bird of special significance to the Persians, became so enamoured of the beauty of the rose that she flew down to embrace it, and in so doing pierced her breast with its sharp thorns. From the drops of blood falling upon the earth there grew the new red roses. According to one Muslim legend, the rose sprang from the beads of sweat of Mohammed. The prophet's companion, Archangel Gabriel, also dropped a bead of sweat which became a red rose. The donkey travelling with them produced the yellow rose. In another legend, roses came not from the prophet but from the perspiration of a lady, Joun, whose skin was white at dawn but rosy at midday. Krüssmann asserts that the Muslims 'would have sought roses with velvety, dark red petals', the Sacred Rose of Abyssinia (*R. richardii*).

Thus it seems that the red rose had particular significance to Christians, and to other religions as well; its propagation followed

This detail from a French calendar of the sixteenth century shows roses on a trellis, with roses being picked so that the lady can make a coronet or garland for her lover.

This medieval manuscript shows a lady making a white rose garland in a turfed, banked rosary, with one of her helpers picking the blooms behind. The word rosary came to be used both for the garden and for the religious form of prayer or set of devotions, the latter not being in common use until the sixteenth century.

not only the flag, but the faith, when Islamic culture swept over Spain and, later, when the crusaders may have brought back roses from the east. The red rose was also important to quasi-mystical groups such as the Rosicrucians. The first documentary evidence for the existence of this curious society is in a tract called the *Fama Tracticus* (1614); Francis Bacon (1561–1626) is said to have been a functionary ('imperator') and to have contributed to the *Fama*. The tract announced the existence of the mystical brotherhood and recounted the journeys of Christian Rosenkreuz, the alleged founder of the order (now believed to have been only a symbolic figure), who acquired on foreign travels wisdom which he imparted to his eight disciples. Other accounts trace the brotherhood's origins back to schools started by Thutmose III in Egypt around 1500 BC. Membership is alleged to have expanded and the brotherhood adopted the symbol of the gold cross with a red rose at its centre. It is thought by others that Paracelsus, a Swiss alchemist, was the most likely founder.

But did such a society really exist? Since it was secret, we shall probably never know. Members are variously called Brothers of the Rosy Cross, Rosy-Cross Knights and the Rosicrucian Fraternity. Certainly there was an English group in 1866, a French group in 1892 and, today, four organized sects in the USA, where the headquarters of the Ancient Mystical Order of Rosae Crucis (AMORC) has its supreme see at San José, California. They claim 250,000 members throughout the world. In 1990, newspaper reports alleged that their leader, Mr Gary Stewart, had been ousted from the order after transferring £2 million of its funds to a bank account in Andorra.

When religion went underground, as in the mysteries of magic and witchcraft, the red rose may have gone with it. Some evidence for this might be assumed from the poem *Rosa Mundi*, published in Paris in 1905 in a limited edition by one H.D. Carr, an alias of Aleister Crowley, the self-proclaimed master of evil. Here is the opening:

> Rose of the World!
> Red glory of the secret heart of Love!
> Red flame, rose-red, most subtly curled
> Into its own infinite flower, all flowers above!

The long poem includes the following passages:

> And thou, O rose, sole, sacred, wonderful,
> Informing all, in all most beautiful,
> Circle and sphere, perfect in every part,
> High above hope of Art . . .
>   . . . Thou art everywhere
> Rose of the World, Rose of the Uttermost
> Abode of Glory, Rose of the High Host,
> Oh Heaven, mystic, rapturous Rose!

Was Crowley deliberately using the religious symbol of the red rose in his own hymn to earthly love, a blasphemy of the kind he was adept at developing in the strange life that kept him out of his native England for long periods? Or was the rose merely a handy symbol of love?

It is not clear why the white rose has less universal significance, except perhaps that there may be an innate fear of its virginal qualities. In *Man and his Symbols*, Jung describes in some detail how the myth 'Beauty & the Beast' expresses the process of female awakening. When Beauty asks her father for a white rose – which he proceeds to steal from the garden of the Beast – this symbolizes her goodness; subconsciously, however, according to Jung, her request puts both her and her father in the power of a principle that expresses cruelty and kindness combined. Undoubtedly 'Beauty & the Beast', which has a white rose at the heart of the tale, is one of the most frightening of children's stories and, as Cocteau showed, can also strike fear into the adult film-going public.

The relationship between religion and the rose may be said to have reached its climax in Victorian England, when the flower came to the attention of Samuel Reynolds Hole. The Rev. Reynolds Hole (as he preferred to be called) was not at all like the namby-pamby clerics encountered in Victorian literature. He was a robust, well-educated democrat whose family had made a fortune in Manchester by, so it was said, 'putting the spots into cotton'. His father was the local squire with a substantial farm at Caunton Grange in Notting-hamshire. As the poet put it, the child is father of the man: something of Hole's character may be judged from the stage instructions to the opening scene of a play he wrote at the age of eight: 'Enter a man swimming for his life'.

After Oxford, Hole became Vicar of Caunton. Then in 1843, at the age of 24, he was suddenly converted not, like some of his Oxford contemporaries, to Roman Catholicism, but to a passionate belief in the power of the rose. In his own words:

> Sauntering in the garden one summer's evening with cigar and book, and looking up from the latter during one of those vacant moods in which the mind is absorbed in 'thinking about nothing at all' my eye rested on a rose.

It was, as a matter of fact, *R.* 'd'Aguesseau' (a Gallica imported in 1833), but the species is immaterial. His passion, a general one, was at first assuaged by a dozen trees, then by two dozen, then a hundred – and soon, his father's land was covered by a thousand roses which in time became four or five thousand.

Hole set out to put the rose at the peak of human endeavour. Rather inclined to use a humorous turn of phrase, he wrote:

> Our warfare in those days was a mere skirmishing, We were only a contingent of Flora's army – the rose was but an item of the general flower show. We were never called to the front . . .

This was in 1859 and already, two years earlier, he had written to the *Florist* magazine suggesting a Grand National Flower Show. The public response was nil, but Hole did not give up and wrote to dozens of prominent rosarians.

In 1858 he had sufficient support to hire not only the St James's Hall for the first Show, but to bring along the band of the Coldstream Guards as an added attraction. This was a mistake and he admitted 'their admirable music was too loud for indoor enjoyment'. The roses were, however, a great success. They arrived by the thousand and a journalist from *The Times* reported that their scent overwhelmed the stench of the nearby Thames. The idea of the Rose Show caught on, and it soon became an annual event. Hole himself was no mean exhibitor – for example, in 1868 he won fourteen first prizes out of sixteen collections shown.

There was, of course, a proselytizing motive to all this. As he explained: 'He who would have beautiful roses in his garden must have beautiful roses in his heart!' Meanwhile, 'the old fox' as he called himself, had caught 'a beautiful pullet' in the shape of the twenty-year-old Catherine whom he married when he was twenty years her senior. By his own admission, the old bachelor had a weakness for falling in love.

Together they set about the Battle of the Roses. Several successful and competent books had been published about rose-growing, but Hole felt they lacked the necessary fanaticism. In 1869 he launched *A Book About Roses*, price seven shillings and sixpence – quite an expensive purchase for those days. It was an instant success and in 1870 a second and third edition were published. It is hard to say why it appealed to the public – Hole's jokes do not seem particularly amusing today and his enthusiasms are somewhat pious. For example, he praises the Nottingham Working Men's Rose Show as an effective means of keeping the poor 'away from the beershops'. Perhaps the Victorians liked nothing so much as a pious thought and Hole could produce plenty of these – 'I have always believed that the happiness of mankind might be increased by encouraging that love of a garden, that love of the beautiful which is innate in us all'. His style was vigorous compared with other gardening writers of his time and he admitted he was writing 'sans étude and therefore sans humbug'.

Hole not only had Catherine's support – there was also that of another cleric, the Rev. Henry Honeywood D'Ombrain, who founded the Rose Society in 1876 at the age of 60. He had been a keen rosarian for many years and is credited with introducing the rose 'Maréchal Niel'. Hole took the chair at the inaugural meeting of the Society in Adelphi Terrace, and is often given the credit for founding it; although Hole was the first President, D'Ombrain did most of the routine work as Hon. Secretary, a post he held for many years. (He died in 1905 aged ninety, a year after Hole.)

Appointed to the Deanery of Rochester in 1888, Hole continued to personify the cult of the rose, lecturing in America, visiting the rose gardens of Nice and its environs, and still finding time for an 'overwhelming' volume of work in church matters. Such was his fame that when he toured the ducal gardens at Belvoir Castle, the head gardener, on learning the name of this distinguished visitor, shouted urgently to the several under-gardeners 'Turn on the fountains! Turn on the fountains!'

In 1901, three years before his death, Dean Hole reflected that in the catalogue from which he had chosen his first dozen roses some fifty years before, which had listed 478 varieties, only eleven were still on the market. He believed, with typical Victorian optimism, that this represented that great virtue Progress. If it did, then Progress continues unabated.

'Ah those Victorian clergymen, theirs must have been a happy existence! Respected and secure, they could not have found their duties arduous, for many were able to devote a considerable proportion of their time to other things'. So wrote an expert on Victorian rose literature, the Canadian Theo Mayer, in an article in the 1970 edition of the *Rose Annual*. He mentions Dean Hole, but observes that while he gets most of the credit, it was the Rev. H. Honeywood D'Ombrain who did 'much of the work in founding the Society. He edited *The Rosarian's Year Book* from 1877 to 1902, and also wrote a little shilling paperback which went through three editions over the same period'. Mayer gives the accolade for 'the best new book to appear in the late Victorian period' to another cleric, the Rev. Andrew Foster-Melliar, whose *The Book of the Rose*

Dean Hole put the authority of the Victorian clergy behind the rose, creating the first National Rose Shows and later playing a leading part in the formation of the Rose Society, now the Royal National Rose Society.

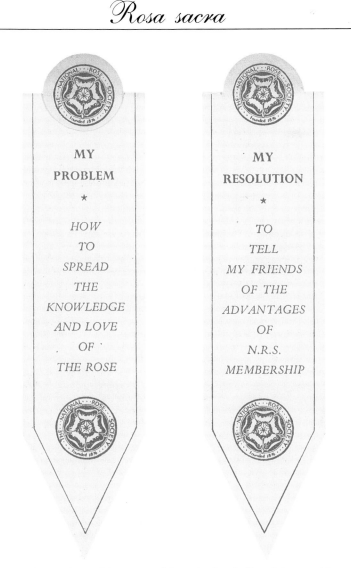

MY
PROBLEM

★

*HOW
TO
SPREAD
THE
KNOWLEDGE
AND LOVE
OF
THE ROSE*

MY
RESOLUTION

★

*TO
TELL
MY FRIENDS
OF THE
ADVANTAGES
OF
N.R.S.
MEMBERSHIP*

The power which members of the National Rose Society believed they could exercise over the world at large is evidenced by the almost religious zeal with with this bookmark enjoins them to recruit disciples from among their friends.

went into four editions between 1894 and 1910, and, he says, is 'still worth reading'.

Today, the most expensive use of the rose in a religious context is probably at funerals. This follows an old tradition. Thomas Christopher suggests that the Mother Goddess (Cybele in Anatolia; Cotytto in Thrace, Corinth and Sicily; Demeter in Greece; Isis in Egypt; Magna Mater in Rome), who always showed a predilection for roses, governed not only fertility but also the afterlife. 'Only through reunion with her, through burial, could man achieve immortality.' He notes that a rose lured Persephone into the grasp of Hades, god of the underworld. Aphrodite anointed the dead

Hector with rose-scented oil to preserve his body from corruption. What was good enough for the gods was good enough for the mortals, and the Greeks and Romans readily wove wreaths of roses for their dead. So did the Egyptians, whose funeral wreath Petrie found in the tombs at Hawara. In the twentieth century, the rose still retains its poignant funeral symbolism. When the pleasure boat *Marchioness* sank in the Thames in 1989, the captain's widow threw a single rose on the waters in memory of her dead husband.

Modern crematoria usually have extensive rose gardens, sometimes very large, like that of the City of London. Alas often there is not enough garden space left to meet the demand; such is the case at Hull crematorium where there is currently a three-year waiting list. Dr Francis Clegg, who has made a study of bereavement, notes that there may be a conflict between the policy of the authorities and the wishes of the bereaved. The latter, finding their specific rose plant bereft of bloom, may not be satisfied with the clinically-pruned spikes preferred by the crematorium's managers. The have been known to decorate the plant with plastic roses, or with stems of roses purchased from a local florist and attached by sellotape. Those authorities who at first found such behaviour unsatisfactory have now, Dr Clegg discovers, come round to the view that the wishes of the bereaved are of paramount importance, and plastic roses have been permitted. Such problems have led the authorities to re-think their policy. Are roses the most desirable type of plant for memorial gardens and is the ever-popular 'Peace' the most desirable rose? There is some movement towards substituting wild flower gardens, at one extreme, or formal Japanese water garden designs, at the other.

Rosa nominata

On 15 December 1989 the family of the late Marjorie Fair celebrated the centenary of her birth. And the event was given some extra interest as the result of the discovery that Marjorie, who had been comparatively unknown except in Hinxworth, North Hertfordshire, where she had lived, had recently become famous in Paris. That she earned this posthumous international reputation was as much due to the game of cricket as anything else. Because it was on the playing field that Jack Harkness, then a young apprentice rose grower but later to become a renowned breeder, first met Marjorie's son Reginald and became a staunch friend of the family. Jack Harkness came to know Marjorie Fair not only as the amiable mother of his friend, but also as a plantswoman and designer who had made one of the finest cottage gardens in the Home Counties. It was these fond memories and a desire to commemorate her achievements which inspired the now-famous Harkness to call one of his best hybrid shrub roses 'Marjorie Fair' 23 years after her death.

The 'Marjorie Fair' rose has massive trusses of bright carmine flowers with white eyes borne on 4 ft. bushes. And Reggie Fair, who had recently retired from schoolmastering and was about to move back into what had been his mother's house, decided that the garden which she had made should contain at least a pair of the roses bearing her name. When he asked at the nearby Harkness nursery whether there were any available, there was some doubt about it because the Directorate of Parks, Gardens and Green Areas of the City of Paris had recently ordered 1450 'Marjorie Fair'. It appeared that the Paris authorities, despite the fact that many of the greatest roses have been bred in France, had chosen these vast quantities of the new English rose because, in the words of their spokesman, 'it is a superb landscaping rose – most suitable for a mass effect. Apart from having beautiful flowers which appear over a long season, it has a splendid general allure'. 'Marjorie Fair' had first come to their attention in 1988 during trials at the 60-acre Bagatelle garden in the Bois de Boulogne. Among the 20,000 roses on show, the Harkness shrub won the first prize in its class. Many of the shrubs ordered by Paris were used for a thick and colourful hedge round the arboretum at the horticultural school in the Bois de Vincennes and the rest were planted in sizeable blocks in different areas of Paris.

PREVIOUS PAGE

The perpetual shrub rose 'Marguerite Hilling' includes the name of its English breeder Hillings Nurseries. It is a sport of 'Nevada', a Moyesii hybrid, itself developed by the Spanish breeder Pedro Dot in the 1920s. This rose was introduced in 1959 after its discovery by Graham Stuart Thomas.

Top The Invitation XI of Monica Dickens, the novelist, photographed at the match in 1950 at which Reginald Fair (right of centre in pads) played against the rose grower Jack Harkness.

Left Harkness, one of Britain's leading growers, was awarded the Order of the British Empire for his contribution to rose breeding.

Above In 1989, Harkness's rose 'Marjorie Fair' became the rage of Paris.

Lower left Harkness was so impressed by the character of Reginald's mother, Marjorie, seen here with her grandchildren, that he named a rose after her.

There is always a temptation to opt for the romantic and, in years to come, unaware of this charming story of why Jack Harkness called his hybrid 'Marjorie Fair', some people will doubtless conclude that she was a woman for whom he cherished a secret passion, or perhaps that she was a mistress he couldn't forget. Once evolved and uttered, such an idea is readily accepted, often cited, and a myth is born. That is why the literature of roses is full of questions about the identity of the ladies after whom roses are named. Vita Sackville-West is typical, when she laments, 'I wish I could find out who Mme Lauriol was in real life to have so sumptuous a flower called after her [the Bourbon 'Mme Lauriol de Barny']. I suspect that she may have belonged to the *haute cocotterie* of Paris of that date.' This is Sackville-West's demure way of suggesting that she was a high-class whore. She goes on: 'Or possibly I misjudge her and she may have been the perfectly respectable wife of some M. de Barny, perhaps a rose-grower of Lyon. Someone ought to write the biographies of persons who have had roses named in their honour'.

Perhaps it is best that such biographies remain unwritten because so often the facts of the case are likely to be disappointing. In 99 cases out of 100 when a breeder gives a rose a female name, it is because he considers it to be particularly pretty and he wishes to honour a woman who is often a member of his family (or someone almost as close, as was the case with Jack Harkness when naming 'Marjorie Fair'), or someone for whom he feels a particular affection, or for whom he feels a particular sense of gratitude, or someone he admires (like Mrs Minniver in the film of that name). It may be his wife, mother or daughter. 'Who were the lovely deep pink 'Marguerite Hilling', the salmon-pink 'Margo Koster', the vivid vermilion 'Anne Cocker' or the scarlet 'Margaret McGredy' named after?' the inquisitive but ill-informed romantic might demand. But they would be far less curious if they knew that their breeders were called Hilling, Koster, Cocker and McGredy. They should also recognize that female names are by far the most popular. Krüssmann made a statistical analysis from a list of modern roses and found the most used to be Madame or Mme (391), Mrs (288), Lady (126), Maria (112), Queen (88) and Frau (39).

It is difficult to determine just what motivates rose breeders when they name their creations after some well-known male or female personality. It could be genuine admiration and this is doubtless often the case. It could be because the name will gain publicity for the rose and increase sales. And it would take a very strong character for a 'personality' to refuse the offer of allowing his or her name to be used for a rose. As is the case with unknown

The 'Evelyn Fison' rose, named after the family of a famous British producer of garden chemicals, is seen here growing in the grounds of Edzell Castle.

names, breeders may christen their creations after public figures because someone has paid them to do it. Whatever the motivation, it has always been one of the ways in which rose hybridists and selectors have identified their roses. 'Adélaide d'Orléans', a pale pink semi-double hybrid of *Rosa sempervirens* raised by Jacques in 1826, and 'Baroness Rothschild', a pink Hybrid Perpetual bred by Pernet in 1868, were just two of the forerunners of a host of more modern roses like Meilland's fragrant Hybrid Tea 'Grace of Monaco', Harkness's orange-red floribunda 'Judy Garland', Buisman's salmon-pink 'Kathleen Ferrier', Curtis's fragrant orange Hybrid Tea 'Lady Bird Johnson' or Tantau's very deep red 'Konrad Adenauer'. There is no doubt that of all the roses named after celebrities there can rarely have been a more affectionate tribute that that paid to the great jazz trumpeter and rusty-voiced singer Louis Armstrong by Sam McGredy when, in 1970, he called his sultry crimson-scarlet Floribunda simply – 'Satchmo'.

The rambler 'Dorothy Perkins' was named by the proprietor of the American rose nursery Jackson & Perkins who introduced it in 1902. The firm is now a giant concern with headquarters in Oregon and was one of many US breeders which had great success with modern roses in the early years of the twentieth century.

Rose growers, like others faced with the need to find an endless stream of names for their novelties, have often been tempted to use the names of military heroes. As recently as 1973, Basildon Rose Growers named its rigidly upright, large and fragrant pink-bloomed Hybrid Tea 'Admiral Rodney', 191 years after that great sailor's resounding victory over the French fleet off Dominica. Meanwhile Generals 'Jacqueminot' (a clear red Hybrid Perpetual from Roussel), 'Kléber' (a deep pink Moss Rose from Robert) and 'McArthur' (a very fragrant rosey red Hybrid Tea from E. G. Hill) presumably commanded by 'Maréchal Niel' (pale yellow Noisette from Pradel) bayonetted their way into the catalogues to ensure that the gallantry of the land forces was not forgotten. Apart from 'Aviateur Blériot', none of the famous aviators, not even Amy Johnson or Lindbergh, seem to have attracted attention.

The heroes of ancient myth, early history and more recent fiction have long provided rose breeders with names for their hybrids, which has helped to ensure the immortality of characters like 'Electra' (a yellow Hybrid Tea bred by Boerner for Jackson and Perkins), 'Merlin' (a golden yellow Floribunda splashed with red from Harkness), 'Minnehaha' (a pink Rambler from Walsh), 'Cleopatra' (a bronze and scarlet Hybrid Tea from Kordes), 'La Tosca' (an early soft pink Hybrid Tea from Schwaartz), 'Long John Silver' (a silvery white climber from Horvath), 'Lilli Marlene' (a scarlet-crimson Floribunda from Kordes), 'Lorna Doone' (a crimson Floribunda from Harkness), 'Robin Hood' (a cherry-red Hybrid Musk from Pemberton) and 'Rob Roy' (a crimson Floribunda from Cocker).

Many rose growers have had retiring personalities and have chosen names for their hybrids which offered no clue to the identity of the breeder. Others have been less reticent. Understandably proud of their achievements, they have unashamedly incorporated their own names into that of the roses which they have bred. 'Paul's Early Blush' (a pale pink Hybrid Perpetual) and 'Paul's Lemon Pillar' (a pale sulphur-yellow climbing Hybrid Tea) resulted from programmes of which George Paul of Cheshunt was particularly proud; 'Paul's Scarlet Climber' (a scarlet Large-Flowered Climber) was a plant which nearby William Paul at Waltham Cross clearly thought was remarkable enough to bear his name. Alec Cocker of Aberdeen was only a mite less lacking in modesty when allowing his bright crimson Hybrid Tea to be called 'Alec's Red'.

It is not difficult to imagine why rose breeders might choose to name their roses after places and there are so many to choose from that the index of an atlas must make a splendid refuge for hybridists whose imagination is beginning to fail. However, the list of places which have so far managed to attract attention is very impressive. It includes: from Meilland – 'Charleston' (yellow-marked crimson Floribunda), 'Monte Carlo' (orange-yellow Hybrid Tea); from David Austin – 'Chianti' (purplish-mauve Shrub); from Johnston – 'Chicago Peace' (darkly veined deep pink Hybrd Tea); from Kordes 'City of Norwich' (crimson-scarlet Hybrid Tea), 'Cologne Carnival' (silvery lilac-mauve Hybrid Tea), 'Hamburg' (deep scarlet Shrub), 'Valencia' (orange-yellow Hybrid Tea); from McGredy – 'City of Belfast' (velvety scarlet Floribunda), 'Galway Bay' (cerise-pink Large Flowered Climber), 'Miss Ireland' (salmon-red Hybrid Tea); from Jackson and Perkins – 'America' (porcelain-pink Climber), 'Cayenne' (deep orange Hybrid Tea); from Dickson – 'Melrose' (creamy yellow Floribunda), 'Manx Queen' (golden-yellow Floribunda); from Harkness – 'Lake Como' (soft mauve

Floribunda); from Tantau – 'Charm of Paris' (clear pink Hybrid Tea), 'City of York' (creamy white Large-Flowered Climber); from Armstrong – 'Taj Mahal' (deep pink Hybrid Tea); from Pernet-Duchet – 'Lyon Rose' (coral red Hybrid Tea); from J. J. Kern – 'Nantucket' (apricot Hybrid Tea). Only rarely has the place where it was first discovered or where the hybrid was created given its name to a rose. Notable exceptions are: 'La Mortola', a highly fragrant white form of *Rosa brunonii*, which was found in 1954 in the famous La Mortola garden near Ventimiglia on the Italian Riviera by its owner Cecil Hanbury, 'Tuscany', a form of *Rosa gallica* with brown-crimson, white-centred petals which is believed to have been first found in the Florence region, and the sport of *Rosa filipes* 'Kiftsgate', the most vigorous climber ever discovered, which Edith Murrell found growing in her Cotswolds garden in 1954.

The most obvious and easy way of christening roses is to include their colour in their name. That is probably why hybridists have adopted the practice and it is remarkable how ingenious they have been in discovering new ways of mentioning the same colour. A quick glance through the catalogue reveals at least 32 names incorporating the word red from 'Red American Beauty' through to 'Red Wings' at the other end of the alphabet. Since red is a colour which is always going to crop up as the result of hybridizing, it is difficult to imagine how future breeders are going to be ingenious enough to find a novel way to include the word in the name. No doubt they will be obliged to adopt the advertising world's favourite adjective 'new', as others have done. Thus 'New American Beauty' and 'New Red Wings'. Pink roses, too, will present problems. The word already occurs followed by 'Cameo', 'Cloud', 'Dawn', 'Favourite', 'Formal', 'Fragrance', 'Frostfire', 'Garnette', 'Grootendoorst', 'Heather', 'Joey', 'Lustre', 'Maiden', 'Mandy', 'Masterpiece', 'Parfait', 'Peace', 'Perpétue', 'Petticoat' (ah well somebody had to do it!), 'Puff' (that, too), 'Ribbon', 'Rosette', 'Shadow', 'Spice' and 'Supreme'. White, also a very common colour, is included in far fewer names. Only two dozen are easy to find. But perhaps that is because plants with white blooms suggest all sorts of other attractive similes with 'Snow', 'Virgin', 'Purity', 'Ice', 'Frost' and 'Maiden' obvious among them.

Examining the names which hybridists have given their roses reveals a strange anomaly. It is almost as though it would be as unlucky to mention the word yellow to a hybridist as it would be to use the word 'Macbeth' instead of the euphemism 'The Scottish play' in front of an actor. Coombes's *Dictionary* shows that while the word 'gold' or 'golden' has been used forty times when christening roses with yellow blooms, the word 'yellow' itself has

The Kiftsgate rose is one of the most vigorous climbers ever bred and was discovered by Mrs Edith Murrell growing in her famous Kiftsgate garden in the Cotswolds. It has become a favourite in many English gardens, although it is inclined to take over its surroundings. Here it is seen on the left at the Old Rectory, Burghfield, Berkshire, a fine garden open to the public.

only been used ten times. Perhaps growers imagine that the word gold or golden evoke a glittering value image which will attract more sales than the word yellow, which has to overcome pejorative associations with disease and cowardice.

All keen rosarians must be grateful to Allen Coombes, who, in researching roses for his *Dictionary of Plant Names*, explained the true meaning and origin of many of the names which seem commonplace in the rose garden. Perhaps the most satisfying feature of Coombes's work is the way in which he translates the Latin specific names which always follow the generic name *Rosa*. These range from *alba* meaning white (*Rosa* x *alba* – white rose) and *canina* – of dogs (*Rosa canina* – Dog rose) to the much more obscure *ecae*, which is derived from the first letters of the name of Mrs E.C. Aitchinson, whose husband introduced *Rosa ecae* to cultivation in Europe from central Asia.

Although Coombes doesn't tell us more about this 4 ft. tall, prickly, yellow-flowered shrub rose from Afghanistan and Turkes-

The Frenchman M. Jacques who raised the famous 'Bourbon Jacques' named this sweet-scented rambler, based on *Rosa sempervirens* 'Felicité et Perpetué' after his two daughters in 1827. Jacques was chief gardener to the Duc d'Orléans and his rose is seen here at Nymans, the garden developed by the Messel family and now in the care of the National Trust.

tan, he does provide the essential spur which sends us scurrying to Dr. Gerd Krüssmann's masterwork *Roses*, in which the former director of the Dortmund Botanic Gardens tells us that Aitchinson was a doctor of medicine who made the introduction in 1880 and that so far there is only one known hybrid called 'Golden Chersonese'.

Few will have difficulty in understanding the shape, colour and geographic origin of a rose when these facts are described by a specific portion of its Latin name. Apart from *alba* there is *versicolor* meaning variously coloured, 'Bicolor' – two-coloured, *xanthina* – yellow-flowered and 'Viridiflora' – green-flowered. Petals are described specifically as *centifolia* – 100 – or 'Trigintipetala' – 30 petals. Leaves can be *nitida* shining, *sericeas* silky or hairy, *glauca* – glaucous, with a bloom on the stem and young leaves – or *rugosa* wrinkled (a feature of the *Rosa rugosa* shrub roses). Roses with *chinensis* as their specific name are clearly of Far Eastern origin and those with *gallica* from France, *damascena* from Damascus (though British rose expert Graham Stuart Thomas suggests that *damascena* might derive from the fabric damask), *persica* from Persia or *omeiensis* meaning from the Omei Shan, China. Other descriptive terminations are *eglanteria* prickly, *elegantula* elegant, 'Persetosa' very bristly, *foetida* smelling of rot, *odorata* scented, *gigantea* very large, 'Mutabilis' very changeable (flower colour), 'Grandiflora' large-flowered, and *pteracantha* meaning with winged spines.

This deliberate mixture of specific names beginning with a lower case letter, and set in italics, and other descriptive names beginning with a capital letter set in Roman script, inside single inverted commas, is not at first easy to grasp. It is used to distinguish between the simple species rose or hybrid found in nature and a particular cultivar or form which has been deliberately selected – and bred by man. Thus *Rosa damascena*, the typical species and *Rosa damascena* 'Trigintipetala', the thirty-petalled cultivar specifically bred for attar of roses.

Hybrids arise when two different species of roses are crossed, either by accident in the wild or deliberately by man. When a rose is known to be a hybrid between two species, its specific name is preceded by a multiplication sign – viz. *Rosa* x *hibernica* which resulted from a cross between *Rosa canina* and *Rosa pimpinellifolia*. The physical appearance of such crosses can vary greatly from the

John Champney was a Charleston rice planter whose hobby was breeding roses of the old 'Noisette' type, themselves named after the French nurseryman Philippe Noisette. Champney was the first American to breed a rose whose fame would continue until the present day. 'Champneys' Pink Cluster' was introduced in about 1811. Tyninghame in Scotland, where this picture was taken, has one of the finest formal rose gardens.

parents. Man-made hybrids, correctly known as cultivars, are created from hand-pollinating selected species and/or hybrids and cloned by grafting. The name of the new rose thus created is always set in Roman type between single inverted commas, as in 'Canary Bird', to distinguish it from a natural hybrid.

Both Allen Coombes and Gerd Krüssmann give many examples of the often exciting and strange stories behind the naming of roses. These include:

> *Rosa banksiae*, an evergreen rose with extremely long and lax thornless stems and small single or double white and single yellow, highly scented flowers or scentless yellow doubles, was found by William Kerr in 1807. It had been in cultivation in China for several centuries under the name Mu Hisiang which means 'grove of fragrance'. It was named in Latin after Lady Dorothea Banks, the wife of Sir Joseph Banks, the noted naturalist who became Director of Kew Gardens. Banks had found Kerr working as a gardener at Kew, and gave him a salary of £100 plus expenses to go to China to work under the auspices of the East India Company with which Banks was connected. When Kerr arrived at the Canton factory he found himself almost a prisoner, as to go any distance in the city was dangerous, and his salary was inadequate to support himself properly. The Chinese despised him. His plant-hunting was confined to three days a month when he was able to visit the Fa-tee gardens (Flowery land) some little way up the river. He managed to send Banks a fine haul of plants, including the Lady Banks's rose, which satisfied his patron sufficiently for him, with the King's permission, to appoint Kerr in 1810 as Superintendent of the Ceylon Botanical Gardens at Colombo, a position he took over two years later. Alas, Banks's patronage was Kerr's undoing, for in 1814 he died, after climbing Adams Peak, of 'some illness incidental to the climate'.

> *Rosa brunonii*, the Himalayan Musk Rose from Western China, a strong-growing climber with corymbs of white flowers, was named after the Scottish botanist Robert Brown who with his brother collected many examples of the wild Scottish Burnet Rose *Rosa pimpinellifolia* in 1793. They grew them in a nursery so as to be able to collect and sow seeds and make selections from the seedlings. This programme yielded at least eight notable varieties.

> *Rosa elegantula*, a pretty pink-flowered shrub rose, was originally called *Rosa farreri* in memory of the autocratic and prolific writer and plant explorer Reginald Farrer who spent

Rosa banksiae was found by the famous plantsman William Kerr in a garden in Canton in 1807 and named after the wife of his patron, the even more famous Sir Joseph Banks.

much time in China. He brought back seeds of this rose in 1915 and gave them to his friend, the famous gardener E. A. Bowles of Enfield, who made selections from the seedlings which led to *Rosa elegantula* 'Persetosa' – 'The Threepenny-Bit Rose'.

Rosa x *harisonii* is named after George Folliot Harison of New York who bred it early in the nineteenth century by crossing *Rosa foetida* with *Rosa pimpinellifolia*. It produced delightful yellow, semi-double blooms and soon became popular all over North America. Early settlers are thought to have taken it with them from New England to the southern and western states. And it is believed that it became the metaphor for a folk heroine of Southern Texas who inspired the popular song *The Yellow Rose of Texas*. The chorus runs:

'She's the sweetest little rosebud that Texas every knew,
Her eyes they shine like diamonds, they sparkle like the dew.
You may talk about Clementine, and sing of Rosalie,
But the Yellow Rose of Texas is the only girl for me.'

Rosa helenae, a very vigorous climber with attractive purplish-red young foliage and flat corymbs of fragrant white, flowers in June and July in the northern hemisphere and was found in central China in 1907 by the English plant-hunter Ernest Henry Wilson, known widely as 'China' Wilson. It was his third expedition to China and his first on behalf of the Arnold Arboretum in Philadelphia, which employed him after he had made two very successful expeditions for the English nurseryman Veitch. Wilson named the rose in honour of his wife Ellen. Unfortunately both were killed in a car accident in Massachusetts in 1930.

Missionaries, while spreading the gospel, often made notable contributions to gardening by sending back seed from the remote places where they worked. Horticulture is indebted to two of them whose names are attached to roses which they discovered. *Rosa hugonis* is a shrub which grows to 8 ft. and prefers dry and stony ground. Its dark brown branches tend to arch and carry characteristic flattened thorns mixed with bristles. The solitary, 2 in. wide flowers, borne on short branchlets, are bright yellow. This splendid rose, which, with *Rosa xanthina*, was a parent of 'Canary Bird', was named after Father Hugo Scallan who sent its seeds back to Kew from western China in 1899. *Rosa moyesii* is an impressive 10 ft. high shrub with elegantly arching red-brown stems, against which pairs of yellowish thorns stand out menacingly. Its medium-large wine-red flowers are graced with prominent golden-yellow stamens which are equally spectacular. It was introduced from western China by the Rev. J. Moyes in 1894 and, as one of the most beautiful species roses, acted as parent to forms like the pink *R. moyesii* var. *rosea*, and the glowing red cultivar 'Geranium' or the wonderful Pedro Dot cultivar 'Nevada' which has very large, almost pure-white double blooms. Another pink-flowered hybrid of *Rosa moyseii*, 'Fargesii', commemorates the name of Paul Guillaume Farges, a French missionary from the Tarn-et-Garonne, who was sent to China in 1867 and remained in north-east Szechwan until 1903. During his career as a botanist he collected some 4,000 dried specimens, which Roy Lancaster in his *Travels in China* notes included several important new ornamental species which E. H. Wilson later collected and sent back to Europe and North America.

As was frequently the case in exploration, the state followed paths which the church had pioneered. And it was close in the footsteps of missionaires from Europe that the Prussian diplomat Doctor Max Ernst Wichura made his way to Japan, from where he sent back two batches of plants of the rose which today bears his name, *Rosa wichuraiana*. This is a very vigorous and hardy rambler which has played a crucial role in many hybridizing programmes. Wichura's first batch in 1861 perished but he was more successful with a second batch which were sent to the Botanic Gardens in Brussels and Munich.

There is nothing immutable about the name of a rose and it is sometimes changed. This may be because the grower has chosen the name of a celebrity who, in retrospect, turns out not to be the popular draw his progenitor believed. Rather more respectable changes are made by botanists for their own good reasons, and in such cases rose-growers' catalogue will usually show a second Latin name in brackets after the given Latin name. The bracketed name is the earlier name.

Few growers believe that the name of a rose alone, even when supported by a highly coloured photograph, is an adequate selling point. The customer has to be enticed into a purchase by further

Rosa moyesii was brought from China in 1894 by the Rev. J. Moyes and is one of the most beautiful species roses. This is the hybrid 'Geranium'.

words. Sometimes these are more-or-less factual, such as 'Beryl Ainger', HT, a sport of 'The Doctor' which was described by its grower Frank Cant as

> Buff yellow, deepening to Golden Yellow at base of petals. Similar habit of growth, form and scent to 'The Doctor'.

This is plain enough, provided the customer is acquainted with 'The Doctor'. Other growers use terminology which would appear to be more at home in a wine list. For example:

> A very pleasing flower of distinct, soft clear colour. Upright, robust.

Sometimes the same rose is given widely differing descriptions in the catalogues of competing rose growers. Mr G. D. Rowley, quoted in the *Rose Annual* of 1956, gives some good examples. The grower Mansfield, writing in 1947, refers to the old hybrid perpetual 'Reine des Violettes' as follows:

> It has been claimed to be the 'blue' rose and is probably the nearest approach that has yet been attained to an object which is quite undesirable.

Another grower, Ellwanger, calls it merely 'muddy', but a third waxes lyrical about the colour:

> One of the rare souvenirs we yet own of the mid-Victorian furore for rich, ripe puces, amaranthes and heliotropes, it is a bold bush of flashing jade bestrewn with richly-perfumed blossoms of amethyst-irised purple.

The palm for poetry, in Mr Rowley's view, must go to the French grower, Francis Meilland, who, writing in 1948, may be translated from his catalogue thus:

> Lovers of the Mediterranean, those who knew the 'veritable folly of light combined with the folly of water' of which P. Valery speaks, will wish to recapture their rapturous memories in this flower. . . . Lovers of the sun who are eternally exiled far from the deep blue skies, at the mention of this name, 'Antheor', will conjure up their images of steep, red rocks, blue sea, lonely creeks, and through this colouring tinge their imaginings with an aura of tangible beauty.

What a disappointment, notes Mr Rowley, to find that in an English grower's catalogue the same rose is dismissed in one line:

> Antheor. Apricot, shaded rose pink. A perfect button-hole.

Rosa ^VI femina

Somewhere in the mists of time past, a man first identified the rose with woman and particularly with female beauty, but he remains as they say in the poetry anthologies, *Anon*. Curiously, the first to celebrate the rose in poetry was not a man but the Greek poetess Sappho who in the seventh century BC called it the Queen of Flowers.

Graeco-Roman civilization was certainly not alone in feminizing the rose. Vishnu, who occupies the second place in the Hindu Triad, and one of whose incarnations was a Krishna, formed his bride Lakshmi from 108 large and 1008 small rose petals. The Persian myths are more complex, with a nightingale becoming enamoured of the white rose named the Queen of Flowers and impaling his breast on her sharp thorns when embracing her, thus producing red roses from the blood which spurted forth. In Malaya, the very word for rose is identical with that for woman. In Muslim legend, the rose sprang from the beads of sweat of the woman Joun, whose complexion was white at the break of day and turned to rosy colour at noon.

It is, however, from the Greeks that Western culture seems to have taken the identification of the rose with femininity. Eos, the rosy-fingered goddess of dawn, left the rose behind as evidence of her first appearance on earth. When Aphrodite, goddess of love, arose from the sea, the foam which covered her nakedness fell to the ground to form white rose bushes. Another legend explains how she also created the red rose when, running to succour her fallen lover, Adonis, who had been gored by a wild boar, she scratched herself on the thorns of a rose bush and her blood turned its white blooms to red. Many ancient story-tellers seemed obsessed with a desire to explain the existence of red roses, which they usually, but not always, attribute to the application of female blood to the white.

Aphrodite's responsibility for the conception of the rose is confirmed by the Greek lyric poet, Anacreon, who lived in the sixth century BC at the court of Polycrates on Samos, one of the largest of the Greek Islands. His Ode 51 is dedicated to the rose and is said by commentators to be the first of its kind, although there must surely have been something earlier by *Anon*. Here is his poem in full; stanza five is notable for its reference to the rosy complexion of the nymphs, another instance of the feminization of the rose.

PREVIOUS PAGE

Empress Joséphine had a considerable effect on rose growing in France. When she died in 1814, her collection was soon dispersed. Thirty years later the French grower Beluze, who had developed a whole series of Bourbon roses, named two of them in honour of the Imperial couple. 'Cendre de Napoleon' came in 1840 when the Emperor's ashes were interred in Les Invalides in Paris, followed in 1843 by this rose 'Souvenir de Malmaison'.

The Spring comes garland bearing,
And wreath and blossom wearing;
And we will aye be singing
The Roses she is bringing,
Come Comrades! songs are ringing
To Summer's Rose! Sweet Summer's Rose.

Like Breath from heaven's own portals
Come Roses bright to mortals;
The Graces sound their praises:
The Loves in flow'ry mazes,
Each one, his voice upraises,
To sing with joy Cithéra's toy.

Plant pleasing to the Muses,
With love all song infuses;
The fragrance from its treasure
It pours with equal measure
On him, whose touch is pleasure,
Or him who strays in thorny ways.

The wise delight and revel
In Roses' bright apparel;
When purple wine is flowing,
When banquets loud are growing
The Rose from colours glowing,
Gives crimson leaves for wine-god's wreaths.

The Dawn is Rosy-fingered;
O'er nymphs have Rose tints lingered;
Love's colour, blooms yet clearer,
On Rosy-hued Cithéra!
What theme, to poets dearer
Than soft Rose light to Goddess bright.

This flower takes off diseases,
In sickness gently pleases;
Its old age cannot sever
The scent it loses never;
And dead, we keep for ever
The perfumed air of Roses fair.

Come! Hear! its birth I'm telling
When Pontus, from his dwelling
Brought forth Cithéra tender;
The blue seas did surrender
Love's Queen, who rose in splendour,
From laughing foam with Gods to roam.

When Zeus his Goddess shewing.
Who, from his brain was growing;
No longer he retained her,
But Queen of War! proclaimed her;

Athéne! Great! he named her;
And forth she came, War-Queen to reign.

The Earth her bloom unfolded,
And sprays of blossom moulded;
Her glowing Roses forming
With colours from the morning,
Made flowers for Gods adorning –
Thus Earth did bear the Rose Gods wear.

(Trans. Mrs Herbert Hills, 1884)

Another Greek legend with feminine connotations concerns Rhodanthe, Queen of Corinth. She was so attractive that admirers followed her around the palace. On one occasion, three of them became too pressing and she fled from her court to the Temple of Diana, where her beauty so enthralled the acolytes of the goddess that Diana's jealousy was aroused. Apollo, Diana's brother, exacted revenge by turning Rhodanthe into a rose bush, and the three suitors into a worm, a butterfly and a gnat.

The emphasis of most of the surviving Greek rose stories is on the immortals, particularly the female, but it can be assumed that in a pantheistic society the mortal female was also believed to have rose-like characteristics. There is negative evidence for this in the report by Solon, the sixth-century BC lawyer, who says that girls who had lost their virtue were forbidden to wear the rose wreath.

In Roman culture, the identification with mortal women seems stronger: the Greek stories about the gods are re-told with major modifications. In the tale of Venus and Adonis, the Romans described how the goddess's lover was killed by the a while hunting; from his blood and her tears there grew the blood-red rose. Another legend tells how Mars, the god of war, developed a passion for Venus and decided to dispose of his rival Adonis. Venus descended to earth to warn her lover of the danger, but in her haste her foot slipped on a rose bush, and from the blood which flowed forth sprang the red rose. Gerard in his *Herbal* of 1633 'reporteth that the Turks can by no means endure to see the leaves of roses fall to the ground, because some of them have dreamed that the first or most ancient Rose did spring of the blood of Venus'; and others of the Mahumetans say that it sprang of the sweat of Mahumet.

The goddess Flora was said to have begged the other gods to come to her aid when she found the dead body of her dearest and most beautiful nymph lying in a glade. She asked them to transform the dead nymph into a new flower, the most beautiful of all. Apollo gave her the breath of life, Bacchus bathed her in nectar, Vertumnus gave her fragrance, Pomona fruit, and Flora herself gave it the final touch, a crowning diadem of petals. Thus the rose became the Queen of Flowers.

While death, blood, and suffering from thorn pricks are essential elements in many Roman myths surrounding the rose, pleasure rather than pain was characteristic of Roman society and the rose – its fragrance, its flavour, its softness and its beauty, all became essential concomitants of that sensuous pleasure. There were, it is true, other symbolic characteristics, such as power, when the rose served as adornment for military men and their chariots as they advanced to war and returned in triumph from victorious battle.

At one point, however, the Roman playboy began to call his playmate *mea rosa* and to present her with the first spring rose. This direct identification with the female, and the sensuousness associated with it, goes well beyond anything that can be found within Greek literature. It may have developed in Roman society simply because the cult of the rose was on such an all-pervading scale. Quite how far the association between the feminine and the rose developed in the Roman mind we shall never know. Certainly no later culture held the rose in such regard.

With the fall of Rome and the temporary decay of its culture, the rose went into decline; rather than being a symbol of feminine beauty and love, it was mainly respected for its remedial properties for the sick. In part this must have been because the early Christians

As Venus was born, the beads of perspiration she shed, according to legend, turned to roses as they fell in the sea. Botticelli painted the scene.

rejected the rose as an obvious symbol of paganism. It was only later that its unconquerable strength was recognized by the Church and, belatedly, adopted. For some centuries, therefore, there is little poetry or art that carried on the Roman tradition connecting the rose and the woman. Not until medieval times was the rose overtly and widely revived in this romantic sense, developing out of the religious poetry which took the classics as its model. References began to blossom, comparing the mouth to a rosebud, the cheeks to rose petals and the rose itself to woman, especially to the Virgin Mary who became the Rose of Heaven.

It would not be correct to suggest that the feminine qualities of rose culture totally disappeared in the post-Roman era. For example, Medardus, Bishop of Noyon in France (475–545 AD), initiated an annual rose festival at which he would give a wreath of roses and twenty gold crowns to the most virtuous maiden in his diocese. Presumably the roses for the garland were taken from his monastery grounds: it is through their continued cultivation in such ecclesiastical institutions that the rose survived and revived.

The earliest medieval gardens were part of the monastic way of life and were usually but not always utilitarian in purpose. For example Benedict, an Italian nobleman, gave up studying at Rome and returned to his home at Subiaco where he established a roseto – little rose garden – 'whose flowers delighted his senses and whose

Martin Schongauer's painting of the Madonna of the Rose Bower (latter half of the fifteenth century) illustrates the thorns as well as the blooms of the Madonna's life.

thorns he used to mortify his flesh'. St Benedict's garden there is still preserved today. He then withdrew to the heights of Monte Cassino where, in AD 530, he established a monastery which formed the model for monastic life for the next 600 years, including its gardening life, with its 'paradises' of flowers and roses. The medieval garden historian, Teresa McLean, says that we need not take this legend of Subiaco seriously. The more sophisticated version takes the origin of the roses back only to 1216, when St Francis of Assisi visited Subiaco, miraculously transforming into roses the bed of thorns which Benedict had set to mortify his flesh. If this version is correct it does not help to explain why, when the Normans conquered England and founded Benedictine abbeys, they established rose gardens across the land. There is a well-known story that when King William Rufus (1056–1100) visited the nunnery at Romsey, with designs upon the twelve-year-old Matilda (future wife of his brother Henry), he gave as his ostensible reason, according to the chronicler, that 'he only wanted to admire the roses and other flowering plants'.

Roses and lilies were the two great devotional flowers of the Middle Ages, and there is little evidence of their popularity in the decorative sense alone. It is even unusual to find records of roses sold to gardeners, as they were from the Earl of Lincoln's house in Holborn, formerly a Dominican monastery, granted to the Earl by Edward I in 1286. One year his income from the sale of roses is recorded at 3s, 2d. Nearby was the Bishop of Ely's town house where he, too, had a rose garden. There was also a rose garden at Westminster. These will have been 'pleasance' gardens and, human nature being what it is, it is inevitable that women of the time would have given rose garlands to their men as they are seen to do in medieval illustrations.

These medieval roses were not like most of the roses grown in gardens today. They were short-lived, blooming only once, notable for their thorns, their cankers, and the contrast between their beauty and their swift and inevitable decay. Thus while the male lover began again, as in Roman times, to portray the object of his affections in the symbolic guise of the rose (as in the *Roman de la Rose* of the early thirteenth century), there developed an equally strong literary and cultural tradition which used the rose to portray the brevity of love and the decay of female beauty.

Edmund Spenser's long poem *The Faerie Queene* (1590–6) is typical of the conventions of his age.

> So passeth, in the passing of a day,
> Of mortal life the leaf, the bud, the flower,
> No more doth flourish after first decay
> That erst was sought to deck both bed and bower,
> Of many a Lady, and many a Paramour:
> Gather therefor the Rose, whilst yet is prime,
> For soon comes age that will her pride deflower:
> Gather the rose of love, whilst yet is time,
> Whilst loving thou mayst loved be with equal crime.

The poets of the next century were to continue to advise young lovers to 'gather ye rosebuds while ye may'. There is an inevitable argument here for *carpe diem*, most eloquently expressed in Horace's *Odes* I. xi.

> What next morn's sun may bring, forbear to ask
> But count each day that comes by gift of chance
> So much to the good.

The first two lines of Shakespeare's first sonnet push the argument straight between the sheets:

> From fairest creatures we desire increase
> That thereby beauty's Rose might never die.

Many more examples of the post-Renaissance poetical passion for roses are given in the chapter on literature. By the eighteenth century, the very word 'rose' had been debased from its medieval religious imagery and its Renaissance literary symbolism to become, according to Partridge's *Dictionary of Historical Slang*, a synonym for the female pudenda or maidenhead. In polite poetry and literature, such crude living speech was avoided and the main emphasis remained on conventional similes, such as cheeks like roses and lips like rosebuds. Below the surface, however, the identification of the rose as the symbol of womanhood prevailed and strenthened.

It was Napoleon who brought about, albeit unwittingly, the much more complete identification between the female and the rose. This was all the stranger because, as far as is known, Napoleon held the rose in no particular regard. Rather the reverse: he refused to use the name Rose which his family and friends applied to his mistress and later empress, Marie-Joséphine-Rose, preferring the simpler Joséphine.

Already widowed, Joséphine had become the mistress of the former nobleman and revolutionary terrorist, Barras: a scurrilous cartoon by Gillray shows her dancing naked in front of him with a similarly unclad member of his harem, both banging tambourines. Barras passed her on to the 26-year-old General Napoleon and, within a few weeks, despite being six years her junior, he was infatuated. 'I awake all filled with you,' he wrote. 'Your image and the intoxicating pleasures of last night allow my senses no rest.' Napoleon and Joséphine found more in common than sensual pleasure alone, but on his side it certainly ranked high. 'She has the sweetest little backside in the world,' he recalled later. 'On it you could see the three islets of Martinique' (from where she hailed).

It is usually said that one of Napoleon's presents to his empress was the château at Malmaison, but in fact he objected to the

One of the most famous of rose growers, the Empress Joséphine, wife of Napoleon I, was born in Martinique and christened Rose.

purchase, claiming it was too expensive, so she found the down-payment and concluded the deal while he was in Egypt. Joséphine later spent millions of francs on the house and garden – all provided by Napoleon. At first the garden was – by Le Nôtre standards – an informal arrangement in the 'English' style. Ironically this was the speciality of a Scot, Blaikie, who travelled in Switzerland and France supplying this fashionable requirement. At the time Joséphine's favourite flower was the tulip; she also brought trees and shrubs from abroad with the aim of supplying the *départements* of France with rare plants for her nurseries. She did not at first spend long periods at Malmaison because, although the garden contained a Temple of Love, Napoleon was not often there. He preferred the more aristocratic Rambouillet. So Joséphine travelled widely, partly to take cures for her alleged infertility and partly to be at Napoleon's side when on campaign.

From 1804, when Napoleon's passion for her was cooling, Joséphine began to spend more time at Malmaison and decided to make roses the major feature of the garden.

It was an unusual thing to do – roses were grown commercially at the time, but there had been no grand private collection. Her plan – a unique one – was to have a sample of every living rose.

Among the roses she grew was the 'Cuisses de Nymphe', known by that name in France since the sixteenth century. 'The thighs of the nymph' is the literal meaning but, as Vita Sackville-West archly remarked, 'I will not insult the French language by attempting to translate this highly expressive name.' Napoleon once told Marshall Bertrand: 'She had the prettiest little sex imaginable,' and perhaps Joséphine thought that by surrounding herself with the symbolic roses she could draw him back to her, despite her inability to provide him with an heir.

It would be misleading to suggest that there would have been no large-scale growing of roses in France without Joséphine. An

Château Malmaison in the days of Joséphine, from a painting by August Garneray. Today it presents a much less rustic vista, and the environs of Paris are slowly encroaching, with a notorious new development not far away.

The gardens at Malmaison today present a sorry comparison with the glory they must have attained under Joséphine's patronage. She is said to have grown well over 200 different species, including 167 Gallicas. Now the house is a memorial to Napoleon, and Joséphine's contribution is neglected by the authorities.

energetic trade had flourished for the previous hundred years, but Joséphine gave it a decisive impetus. Gallica is the name associated with France and the oldest of garden roses in Europe. They are known to have been cultivated in several varieties in the early seventeenth century, when the Dutch were raising seedlings to produce new types. The French took up this activity on a big scale and it was at this time that the name Gallica became accepted. The same rose was also called Rose of Provins. Austin, the famous English grower, describes it as usually a shrub, generally not more than 4 ft. in height, of strong upright growth and with numerous small bristly thorns. The leaves are oval, pointed at the top, rather rough-textured and often dark green. The flowers are held singly or in threes and the buds are spherical.

Quite early in her rose-collecting days, Joséphine got to know André Dupont, the foremost rosarian of France, who had a nursery at Rue Fontaine-au-Roi. It is generally agreed that Dupont was the first man to make carefully planned crosses by hand pollination, the process explained in the chapter Rosa Mutabilis. (Most of his colleagues relied on honey bees to do the pollination for them.) He knew and introduced Joséphine to a number of prominent rose growers of the time, not only in France but as far afield as Brussels. She also engaged the services of a botanist, M. Ventenat. Despite the fact that her country and her emperor were at war with England, Joséphine persuaded Napoleon to provide a passport for one of her gardeners, the Irishman John Kennedy, to enable him to pass freely through the British and French lines in order to buy roses and return with them to France. In Britain, the Prince Regent issued special passports so that British experts could work for her. A French expert, Jean Gaijard, says that as early as 1801, the British sent Joséphine Bengal Roses and 'in 1810' *R. indica* (*R. chinensis*).

Napoleon continued to support her financially, even after their divorce in 1809, when he sent an extra 100,000 francs so that she could plant whatever she liked. In its prime, Joséphine's garden contained 167 types of Gallica roses, 27 Centifolia, 3 Moss, 9 Damasks, 22 China, 4 Pimpinellifolia, 8 Alba, 3 Foetida and a number of others. Identifying them all was not easy, even though there were far fewer roses than today, as there were more names than varieties. Some individual roses had as many as fifteen different names because the French growers gave roses from Holland, often un-named, their own names. Joséphine herself was an active namer of roses; some which she chose support the theory that her passion for roses was a subconscious expression of sexual love for the man she was losing – and was to lose because she could not have his children. First there was 'L'Empéreur'. Then 'Cuisse de Nymphe Enuié', 'Belle Aurore', 'Le Feu Amoureaux' and 'Le Rosier des Dames'. Another name for the Cuisse rose was 'La Séduisante', the Seductress.

A rose named after Dupont, *Rosa dupontii*, may have been raised at Malmaison. It appears in Redouté as *R. damascena* var. *subalba*, although we must remember that Redouté's rose book was made up of paintings made over a number of years and published as a series of prints from 1817–24, beginning therefore three years after Joséphine's death. He may have used other gardens and nurseries to find roses to paint. Austin describes this species rose as about 3 in. across and single, white, sometimes tinged with blush, and held in nice Damask-like sprays of five or more blooms. It grows as a strong and rather loose shrub of perhaps 7 ft. in height.

Joséphine aroused public interest in roses by encouraging rose growers and prominent public figures to visit her garden. In the last year of her life, when Napoleon could no longer help her and she was worried about debts, Czar Alexander of Russia, Napoleon's enemy and conqueror, visited her to offer patronage. When he left, she took a rose from a vase for him, saying it was 'un souvenir de

These murals in the Château de Malmaison depict the Cortège de Venus whose flower was, of course, the rose. They show (A) The dance, (B) The music and (C) The triumph of Cupid, who places a garland of roses over the head of Venus.

Malmaison'. About thirty years later, in 1843, a Lyon grower used the name 'Souvenir de Malmaison' for a new Bourbon.

When Napoleon's era came to an end, Malmaison, like the rest of Paris, was faced with a British take-over. A well-known grower, Jean-Paul Vibert, whose mentor, a M. Descemet, had bred 10,000 seedlings from Joséphine's roses, decided to take the stock to his own grounds, where they were the basis for some 600 hybrids of fine quality which he sold widely to those who wanted them, including the British. One member of the British aristocracy purchased 1000 bushes in a single order. The French writer Jean Gaujard gives a different story. Writing in the *Rose Annual* (1950), he says that in 1813 Joséphine's collection of 218 species or varieties was purchased by the French government and exhibited in the Luxemburg Gardens.

Historians are in no doubt that Joséphine's garden became a focal point for the development of the rose in France. She had made it an essential French flower. The statistics suggest her remarkable influence. Five years before she began her work, a leading Paris nursery was offering for sale a mere 100 rose species. She herself collected over 250 at Malmaison. Twenty years after her death, a leading Parisian nursery was listing over 2500 varieties and by 1900 the French national rose museum, Rosérie de l'Hay, listed 3000.

Joséphine's roses are probably best known through the work of Redouté. In his day he was probably thought of more as a botanist than a painter. However, he did study painting at the Jardin du Roi in Paris, and there met a keen amateur botanist whom he followed to London. There he met the famous Sir Joseph Banks and, more significant for his future, learnt stipple-engraving.

On his return to France, Redouté became renowned for his skill in painting plants and at one time had amongst his pupils and patrons two queens and two empresses. Joséphine employed Redouté to record her collection of plants and so became one of his distinguished line of patrons. His method was to prepare water-colours on vellum for presentation to his patrons and – perhaps – for later publication. At first, he himself engraved plates for publication using the new stipple method, but later, as he became more established, he seems to have given up engraving and left it to others. It is not true to say that Redouté's published watercolours feature only roses from Joséphine's collection alone, but there seems no doubt that her patronage was important to his development as a rose painter. Redouté's book of the roses, which included some 170 of the varieties said to be grown at Malmaison was published between 1817 and 1824. Redouté lived on until 1840, but his final years were clouded by financial difficulties.

Naming roses after women is a fashion which seems to have developed following Joséphine's death. It continues today. In one sense, the more notable the woman, the more useful her name to the rose grower. Of the Gallicas, there was the 'Duchesse d'Angoulême', bred prior to 1827, the 'Duchesse de Montebello' prior to 1829 and the 'Duchesse de Buccleuch' introduced in 1846. As for the rose called 'Empress Josephine' (no accent), this only acquired its name quite recently, although it is one of the most beautiful of the old roses. It is pink, very feminine and would probably have met Napoleon's criterion for beauty in the most intimate parts of the female form. Alas, it has no more than a faint fragrance.

Another woman whose name will be as well remembered as Joséphine's in rose history is the Duchess of Portland. Her husband, the 3rd Earl, inherited his title from a Dutch grandfather who had arranged the peaceful revolution of 1688 by organizing the arrival of William of Orange on English shores. The Portland rose was revolutionary, too. It was repeat-flowering. Its origins are unknown, but it was first found in the famous nurseries (founded by the Romans) at Paestum, south of Naples, in about 1780. The Portlands were in Italy on the Grand Tour at the time, and Lady

Left Marie Antoinette as a peasant, a portrait which caused considerable protest when Vigée Lebrun painted it, for it was considered that the Queen was not grandly enough dressed. The roses she is holding may have encouraged Joséphine to think of roses as regal.

Right Pierre-Joseph Redouté (1759–1840) is often called, 'the Raphael of the Rose'.

Portland heard about the discovery and acquired the rose to bring back to England. A cutting was sent to France by the Duchess. This came into the hands of Joséphine's friend, Dupont, and it appears likely that he first gave the rose its name. One difficulty about this story is that, according to Anny Jacob, the Portland rose was available in England as early as 1775.

The French quickly recognized its importance and there were soon 150 different varieties of Portland Rose on the market in Paris. The original rose was bright scarlet, but some of the important varieties were coloured differently, for example 'Rose Lelieur' of 1812 (bright red and violet), 'Coeline Dubos' of 1849 (bright pink) and 'Blanc de Vibert' 1845 (white). By 1850 most of the varieties in France had been overtaken by the new Bourbons and then by the Hybrid Perpetuals. In England, however, there were eighty-four varieties growing at Kew, of which a handful remain today in smaller gardens. Graham Stuart Thomas describes its structure, with the leaves packed tightly round the flowers, as a rosette or shoulder of leaves. These small, compact shrubs have a strong Damask fragrance and, says Austin, can be relied on to provide flowers later in the year. Incidentally Lady Portland is also immortalized by the Portland Vase, now in the British Museum, which she bought in Italy on a visit to Sir William Hamilton, Emma's husband.

Proof of the continuing popularity of the feminine-named rose is the frequency with which they appear in the latest edition of the most popular rose book of all time, David Hessayon's *Rose Expert*, which has sold well over three million copies. About one fifth of the varieties he lists have female names (examples are given in the chapter Rosa nominata).

Certain women will always have rose associations – Constance Spry, Maud Messel, Ruby Fleischmann, Anastasia Law, Vita Sackville-West at Sissinghurst and Heather Muir at Kiftsgate. Before pursuing such connexions, it is interesting to return once more to France to follow the subconscious identification that developed (or perhaps was always there) between the rose and the female form.

Many French painters of the nineteenth century painted the rose, but perhaps none so conspicuously as Renoir. He came from a working-class family and, while he later moved in higher grades of society, he retained many working-class attributes. In fact he began life as an apprentice porcelain painter, putting roses on plates and vases, but the trade deteriorated as machine-painted goods destroyed the market for the hand-painted variety. Although he became successful as a painter, he insisted that he worked for pleasure, and women became almost central to that pleasure. He told his friend André, 'Painting is done to decorate walls. . . . For me a picture – we are forced to paint easel pictures – should be something likeable, joyous and pretty – yes, pretty.'

Success meant he could paint 'pretty' pictures, paintings of the female form and, coupled with these, the rose. 'He particularly associated roses with the beauties of the female body,' says the critic John House. Consider *The Concert* in which two young ladies sit surrounded by roses – in their hair, their hands and in the fabrics about them. 'The rhythms and echoes between the objects create a

Renoir always used the rose to establish the essential femininity of his women, as in the famous *La Loge* where the rose in the bosom is the focal point.

Gabrielle, Renoir's favourite model, draws the viewer's attention to the rose at her ear. It was probably a Bourbon, but the variety is immaterial.

series of metaphysical associations,' says House. 'No one object is simply equated with another, but all become part of a single chain of connexions, and all celebrate a set of interrelated values; the physical splendour of young women, the richness of materials and gilded surfaces, the lavishness of flowers and their associations with the sense of smell'.

The 'lavishness of flowers' was best displayed by the rose. In conversation with Vollard, Renoir associated roses with the physical beauties of the female body and, in particular, with those areas with an overt sexual association. In his famous theatre painting, *La Loge*, the rose in the coquette's bosom, with its heavy flesh tones, is symbolic of what would be seen if the coquette were undressed. Renoir's more directly erotic paintings of women, like those of Gabrielle, show the female form more openly than in *La Loge*, but our attention is focussed on the rose at her ear, a fairly explicit symbol. John House points out the 'warm reds which link her cheeks and lips to the roses'. Studies of roses might, Renoir told Vollard, act as 'researches in flesh tones which I make for a nude'. After 1900, says House, as Renoir adopted a fuller, more mature vision of female beauty, he focussed on the rose, with its fullness of form, as an attribute of this beauty. In Renoir's full frontal nudes, such as *Femme nue couchée*, he drapes the secret parts of his model's body but once again directs our attention to the rose at her ear. It is Gabrielle again, given a hint of exoticism by the elaborate cushions and the rose.

Renoir's roses are not easy to identify in botanical terms. They are rich, Bourbon-type, sensuous blooms which we know have a heavy scent even though we cannot smell them. Renoir probably told his models to go into his garden to pick the roses they would pose with. We do not know what kinds he grew, but they were perhaps Bourbons or Hybrid Perpetuals. The Bourbons were immensely fashionable in France at the time and his very painterly blossoms could well be a representation of their feminine charm.

Renoir's Bourbons are more sensuously feminine than the simpler, earlier roses which decorate the work of the Renaissance

Carolyn Fenwick, a typical English rose.

painters – for example, those which shower down on the Venus being born out of the sea in Botticelli's picture, said to be *R.* x *alba* var. *semiplena*. It may be that the very botanical development of the rose and the search for fuller growth, stronger colour, greater variation in colours in the single bloom and greater fragrance was itself a result of its (by now full-blown) feminine connotations.

With the twentieth-century passion for more and more varieties of rose, the fashion for naming them after women continued undiminished. So, too, did the name Rose. Somerset Maugham's Rosie in *Cakes and Ale* and Laurie Lee's Rosie are more feminine by being so named and nothing could be more evocative than Dylan Thomas's Mae Rose Cottage who, very close and softly drawing out the words, says:

> Call me Dolores
> Like they do in the stories.

She must have felt that, by the 1950s, Dolores was an even more glamorous name for a seventeen-year-old who boasted 'I'll sin till I blow up!'

The description 'an English rose' to denote a certain type of English female beauty, mainly facial beauty, or beauty of expression, seems to have been used in the eighteenth century to describe the creamy-skinned, rose-cheeked women painted by Gainsborough, Reynolds and others. The description continues to the present, and *The Times* of 30 March 1990 quotes the actress Jane Asher as believing it aptly applies to a 'blonde, pale-skinned, eighteen- or nineteen-year-old, demure, wearing a floaty flowering dress, drifting through the fields, blowing the down off a dandelion, blushing as a gentleman crosses the fields towards her, with a hint of the purity not being steadfast; there's fire below the ice'. Miss Asher is reported to have added that the rose itself is 'desperately romantic and, as with the girl, it promises eventual fulfilment'. Quite what this last sentence means must be left to the English roses to decipher. Botanically, it is balderdash.

The femininity of the rose has not, curiously, prevented its being used with a masculine connotation on occasion. One of the best-selling songs of the American writer, Frank L. Stanton, made famous by Al Jolson, goes:

> Sweetest li'l fellow, everybody knows;
> Dunno what to call him, but he's mighty like a rose.

Somehow the rose seems able to take on all these rôles without loss of an essential association with the female of the species.

VII
Rosa amatoria

Love is a sticky subject and many an encyclopaedia reflects the difficulty by devoting more space to lunacy than to love. We cannot be sure what an ancient writer meant when he used the word which is translated as 'love'. Aristotle seems to have arrived at a more down-to-earth definition than Plato, but what did the Greeks mean by their use of the word when applied to their deities?

Aphrodite, Greek goddess of love, created the rose according to myth, and the rose appears to have had some association with love from early times. For Sappho, it was Queen of the Flowers; one of the most distinguished of Greek scholars, Professor Sir Hugh Lloyd-Jones of Oxford, admits, however, that 'the society Sappho lived in is a mystery to us'. The fragments of her poetry which survive are almost all thought to be quotations used by other poets. They include a reference to one of her lovers as 'Rosebud', and to another's bosom as 'rose-like'.

Anacreon's Ode 51, said to be the first poem dedicated to the rose, mentions love but we cannot be sure what the poet meant when he wrote:

> Plant pleasing to the Muses
> With love all song infuses.

We can be clearer about the rôle of the rose when reading Philostratus' letters to young men – frank examples of the Greek pursuit of homosexual love for boys above the age of puberty. He writes to one such lover, asking him to return the roses he had sent him and which he had strewn over his bed 'since they then will have not only the smell of roses but also the fragrance of your body'. Other letters to boys also concern roses:

> (1) . . . These roses desire with longing to come to you, and their leaves as wings carry them to you. Receive them kindly as a memorial of Adonis, or as the purple blood of Aphrodite, or as the choicest fruits of the earth. The crown of olives adorns the athlete, the flowering tiara a great king, the helmet a warrior; but the rose is the ornament of a beautiful boy, since it resembles him in fragrance and in colour. It is not you who will adorn yourself with roses, but the roses themselves with you.
> (2) . . . I have sent you a crown of roses, not (or at least not exclusively) to give you pleasure, but out of affection for the roses themselves, that they may not fade.

PREVIOUS PAGE

Although 'Rosa Mundi' is often said to have been named after the unfortunate mistress of Henry II, Fair Rosamund, in the twelfth century, this seems doubtful as it was mentioned by name only in 1581, and nothing is known of its origins. A Gallica rose, it is also known as 'Versicolor'.

According to the latest research, this picture of Venus, Cupid, Folly and Time by Agnolo Bronzino (1503–72) is not a simple allegory but a sermon on the subject of venereal disease. Several of the protagonists are holding roses.

(3) . . . The Spartans clad themselves in purple-coloured garments, either to frighten their enemies by the obtrusive hue, or in order that they might not see when they were wounded, owing to the resemblance of the colour to blood. So must you beautiful boys arm yourselves only with roses, and let [those] be the equipment that your lovers present to you. Now the hyacinth suits a fair-haired boy well, the narcissus a dark one, but the rose suits all, since once it was itself a boy. It infatuated Anchises, deprived Ares of his weapons, enticed Adonis. It is the hair of spring, the brightness of the earth, the torch of love.
(4) . . . You reproach me for not having sent any roses. I omitted to do so, not from forgetfulness, not from want of affection, but I said to myself, you are fair and beautiful and on your cheeks the roses bloom, so that you need no other beside . . . . Also this flower is of a sorry kind, for its

appointed time is only brief, and it soon fades away, and, as we are told, the first beginning of its existence is melancholy. For the thorn of a rose pricked Aphrodite as she passed by . . . . Yet why should we not crown ourselves with the flower which spares not even Aphrodite?

If the rose was an erotic symbol of homosexual love, it must also have been put to the same use in heterosexual wooing. Aristophanes used the word in a general way when he said 'You have spoken all things beautifully of me by referring to me as 'rose-like''. A more specific use was by Pherecrates, a comic writer of the fifth century BC roughly contemporary with Aristophanes, who used the word rose to mean the female pudenda.

Roman writers make a much clearer link between roses and love than the Greek. For example, Apuleius's *Golden Ass* written in the second century AD, as translated by Robert Graves, tells how the princess Psyche had 'rose garlands presented to her by an adoring crowd of supplicants who address her by all the titles that really belonged to the Great Goddess of Love herself'. Later, the story has a happy ending when she weds Cupid, son of Venus, at a great breakfast where the Hours 'decorated the palace with red roses and other bridal flowers'. The red rose was preferred to the white for its obvious symbolism, the white rose connoting virginity.

The identification of the rose with physical love cannot be traced with any certainty to an earlier period than this. True, it had been used in the rites of worship of Aphrodite in Greek times. The rose used for this purpose on the Island of Samos was the Autumn Damask, the only rose to have the ability to repeat-flower until the China Rose was introduced to Europe in the eighteenth century. When the Damask spread to mainland Greece and then to Rome, it continued to be used in ceremonies of a sacred nature, this time connected with Venus. It is not at all clear what function the rose fulfilled, but there is no evidence that it was explicitly sexual.

So even in Roman times, the rose seems to have been more of a decorative accompaniment to an orgy rather than an essential part of it. Those engaging in Bacchanalian rites employed other symbols of an explicitly sexual kind. The phallus and the flagellant painted on the walls of the Villa of Mysteries at Pompeii, even though veiled to conceal their full impact, are clearly intended to be essential tools of the trade in the ceremonial. The rose played no part in all this and it was probably its assumed medicinal properties which kept it, in modern parlance, 'clean'. The painted roses which survive on the walls of Pompeii appear to be decorative in purpose.

Other cultures also link the rose with love. Hafiz praised the rose and Akbar's son, great-grandson of the famous gardener

The Lay of the Nibelungen, written in Strasburg in about 1420, shows the monk Ilsan and his friend the knight being kissed by their respective ladies, all under the influence of roses.

Baber, made a Garden of Delight for his wife in Kashmir, which included roses. Again we cannot be sure whether there is any erotic element here. Incidentally, it is believed that the gardeners in Kashmir may have produced a recurrent rose as a result of continuous reselection, and from Kashmir came the Hundred-petalled Rose. The romance of the nightingale and the rose was a favoured subject for the Persians and, as noted later, was a subject which appealed to Oscar Wilde.

By the Middle Ages there is a more explicitly sensual element in some rose-love references. In an illustrated manuscript on roses written in Strasburg *c.*1420 (the lay of the Nibelungen) one of the illustrations shows a man surrounded by roses being kissed by a lady, while his companion receives a garland from another. Similar illustrations in that other famous illuminated manuscript, the *Roman de la Rose*, are also used by experts to link romantic love and roses, but it is unlikely that this was the author's intention – although it may have been that of his anonymous illustrators. Eva Dierauff quotes a verse from the Middle Ages which reads: 'Maiden may I go with thee to thy rose garden? I would lead thee, sweet love, to the place where the red roses grow.' This might indicate that he had designs on her virginity.

It seems clear to scholars that the original French poem *Roman de la Rose* is not concerned with love, romantic love, in the way the word is used today. The 4000 lines of the poem – whose title means 'the story of the rose' – were composed by Guillaume de Lorris between 1225 and 1237. It was not written for publication in the modern sense and was first circulated in manuscript copies and not printed until well over two hundred years later.

The 'love' which is central to the poem is the doctrine of courtly love developed by the Provençal troubadours. Briefly, they were lyric poets of the twelfth and early thirteenth century, writing – for the first time in Europe – in their vernacular tongue, who achieved such fame that their language was adopted as the standard for lyric composition by other European writers.

The troubadours travelled the courts of Europe where they were welcomed as creative poets and singers. Their theme of courtly love was probably drawn from Ovid, from Platonic doctrine transmitted by Arab and Christian philosophers and

The huge rose-bud on the right is being shown by Bel-Acueil, the hero of the *Roman de la Rose*, to his lover. This illustration is taken from the Harley MSS in the British Library.

idealized forms of love from Hispano-Arabic poets. They were instrumental in developing a code similar to that of the initiation of the knight in feudal society, where the submissive lover sought his reward in the devotion and service offered to the lady rather than through physical love. 'His reward came from the improvement of his *valor* or inherent worth, and his *pretz* or reputation. . . . Although the troubadour's love song was addressed to his lady, it was concerned with the joy or despair of the singer'. Eventually (in the fourteenth century), the lady was replaced by the Virgin Mary and the theme of courtly love faded.

This is the background to de Lorris's poem, written at the height of troubadour fame. The poet describes a dream in which he is admitted to the Garden of Love where he finds courtly virtues personified, while the vices (Hatred, Envy, etc.) are excluded from the Garden. His guide into the garden is Lady Idleness, who wears a rose garland and who introduces him to Sir Mirth, who also wears a rose chaplet. Mirth and his friends are dancing on the grass and several of them have garlands or chaplets of roses. The poet falls in love with the Rose which is the symbol of the courtly lady and the lady's love. First he has to listen to the precepts of the God of Love whose clothes are decorated with roses. Then the progress of his love is described in an allegory in which the feelings of the lady are personified by *Bel Accueil, Dangier, Petié, Male Bouche*, and so on. His own doubts and desires are personified in *Nature* and *Raison*.

The poet presumably chose the rose as his symbol because of the tradition in classical poetry which brought together the rose and love, although a very different kind of love from that which he describes. When he died, de Lorris's poem was unfinished. It was continued some 40 years later by a poet who held very different ideas, Jean de Meung of Paris. He was a man of 'the schools', brought up in the tradition of Aristotelian thought who despised the concept of courtly love as contrary to the spirit of Nature. To such a rationalist, courtly love was deceptive and illusory and to him love existed in order to propagate the species.

Accordingly, in the part of the poem which he added, the tower in which Bel Accueil is imprisoned is taken by storm and the lover allowed to pick the Rose, presumably a metaphor for taking his lover's virginity. In fact the poem, under de Meung's hand, becomes a vehicle for digressions about the various ideas of man and the universe current at the end of the thirteenth century, as well as a satire about women rather than an eulogy of them.

The *Roman* was immensely successful, both as a manuscript illustrated with pictures and later as a printed book, which had gone into 40 editions by 1538. An English version, mostly of the earlier

Illustrations in the *Roman de la Rose* emphasize the rose theme in the margins.

de Lorris text, appeared in the 1370s: the first 1700 lines are ascribed to Chaucer. Skeat, the great Chaucerian scholar, says that Chaucer was very familiar with the *Roman* and often quoted it in his poetry, but his actual translation (if it was his) did not appear in print until 130 years after his death. It has little of the verve and life of Chaucer's own poetry – and, even if it is only a translation, it seems curiously flat.

The following lines from Skeat's edition of Chaucer are quoted verbatim, rather than in a modern version, but readers unfamiliar with Chaucer should not be put off. Read the words aloud and all the old spellings will quickly make their meaning clear, except perhaps for one or two words which have no direct contemporary equivalent, such as *knoppes* whch means heads or buds.

In thilke mirour saw I tho,
Among a thousand thinges mo,
A ROSER charged ful of roses,
That with a hegge aboute enclos is.

Toward the roser gan I go.
And whan I was not fer therfro,
The savour of the roses swote
Me smoot right to the herte rote

Of roses were ther gret woon
So faire wexe never in roon.

I love wel swiche roses rede;
For brode roses, and open also,
Ben passed in a day or two;
But knoppes wilen fresshe be
Two days atte leest, or three. . . .

Might I a gerlond of hem getten. . . .

Among the knoppes I chees oon
So fair, that of the remenaunt noon
Ne preyse I half so well as it,
When I avyse it in my wit.
For it so wel was enlumyned
With colour reed, as wel y-fyned
As nature couthe it make faire,
And it had leves wel foure paire

Until Rabelais' bawdy book, *Gargantua and Pantagruel*, no story in French was so widely known and read in Europe as the *Roman*. Whatever de Lorris's intention, the symbolism of the rose as the lady appealed to the baser instincts of his male readers. When the first illustrated manuscript appeared about 60 years after de Lorris's death, with the added text, the illustrations were perhaps of more than usual significance. The woodcuts on this page appeared at the end of the fifteenth century (well over 250 years after de Lorris's death), and the eagerness with which the lover gazes at the rose is evident in them all. The illuminated manuscripts show an even more sophisticated relationship between the lover and the rose.

Other dream books followed the success of the *Roman de la Rose* and, in the fifteenth and sixteenth centuries, there was widespread literary and pictorial use of the rose as the symbol of love. Quite how many different meanings the rose symbolized in terms of 'love' it is impossible to say. For example, the sixteenth-century English chronicler, John Stowe, relates the legend of Fair Rosamund, mistress of Henry II (1133–89). She was murdered by his queen, Stowe suggests, and 'when she was dead she was buried at Godstone in a house of nunnes, beside Oxford', with these verses on her tomb:

Hic jacet in tumba Rosa Mundi, non Rosa Munda.
Non redolet, sed olet, quae redolere solet.

Peter Coates translates this as:

Here rose the graced, not rose the chaste, reposes.
The scent that rises is no scent of roses.

The striped Gallica 'Rosa Mundi' is believed to have been named after this unfortunate woman of the world. But did her epitaph, if accurately recorded by Stowe, imply that the rose was already used to symbolize a female who had pursued the arts of love? By the Renaissance, the convention was by now an established one, and henceforth the rose would be a symbol of short-lived sexual love. The Herrick poem known to us all as 'Gather ye rosebuds' is in fact entitled *To Virgins, To Make Much of Time*. Another poem by Herrick, *How Roses Came Red*, emphasizes the erotic element.

> Roses at first were white,
> Till they co'od not agree,
> Whether my Sappho's breast,
> Or they more white sho'od be.

Roses feature powerfully in Boucher's portrait of his patron Madame de Pompadour, mistress of Louis xv. Boucher also painted nudes, and his *Reclining girl* has a rose in a provacative position.

The picture of Madame du Barry as the goddess Flora was painted by François Drouais (1727–75). A rose was named after her, the Rose du Barry, and her bedroom was decorated with roses, as were some of her most lavish dresses. It is possible that the Empress Joséphine took her as a model.

The European rose itself was still both red and white, and of the short-flowering variety, until the repeat-flowering China or Tea roses which appeared here in the eighteenth century. These bloomed recurrently, not only in Europe, but also in America and other parts of the world where the only roses had formerly been short-lived – hence the now universal decline of the rose as a symbol of quick death and the brevity of love.

With the arrival of the bushier, longer-flowering blooms, the rose's marriage with love took on a steadier tone. Louis XV's mistress, Madame de Pompadour, was seldom painted without a rose; Sacheverell Sitwell follows other authorities in claiming 'Belle de Crécy' as a rose to be found growing in her garden. 'The scent of it takes you in a breath into the eighteenth century, while the rose

Richard Strauss's opera *Der Rosenkavalier*, completed just before the outbreak of the First World War, has been described as the last grand opera of the Old World. It is constantly being revived, and in 1980 the Glyndebourne company commissioned the famous designer Erté to work on a new production. This is his sketch of the young lover whose ostensible rôle is to act as a messenger carrying the symbolic rose.

pink petals and jade green leaves make one think of the bows and ribbons of the Pompadour by (the painter) Boucher'. In fact, her garden was fuller of hyacinths than roses and at the Trianon two million pots of them were kept for bedding out on the parterres at Versailles. Madame du Barry gave her name to the colour Rose du Barry. Her bed at Versailles had a canopy of roses, with silk curtains embroided with the same flower. She was painted by Drouais as the Goddess Flora.

Once the rose had lost its association with short life, it was possible for a lover to give his amour a bouquet of roses and imply that they were symbolic of eternal love. A twentieth-century opera, which looks back to eighteenth- and nineteenth-centry values, illustrates the point. It is based on the legend of the *Rosenkavalier* or the Knight of the Rose who takes the silver 'bloom' to the chosen bride. Kobbé, writing about Richard Strauss's opera, refers to this as the 'customary symbol' which is presented to the bride not by her suitor, but by a messenger on his behalf. In the *Rosenkavalier*, the messenger, young Oktavian, falls in love with the potential bride. Here is von Hofmannsthal's libretto:

Oktavian: I have the honour, in the name of my noble cousin Von Lerchanan (Baron Ochs) to present the rose of Love to his bride.

Sophie: I am grateful to my Lord....It has a strong scent . . . Like a real rose.

Oktavian: There is Persian attar in it.

Sophie: It is like a rose from Paradise . . . . Do you not think so too? . . . it is like a greeting from Heaven . . . unbearably sweet . . . . It tugs my heart strings.

Portrait of Monsieur Germain (1900) by Renoir. In Monsieur Germain's day, no gentleman would have been seen without a buttonhole, but today, alas, the buttonhole is on the wane.

It is clear that the two young people (who have never met before) are already in love. The bitter-sweet duet which follows tugs at the audience's heart strings, too. Music and theme are so powerful that, since it was first performed in Dresden in 1911, no German opera has had so many public performances. This popularity reflects the immense power of the rose as the symbol of love, not only for the young people but also, in a different sense, for Oktavian's lover the Marschallin, who, like the rose, is past her prime and must pass on the *Rosenkavalier* to a younger female.

When a man gives a rose to a woman, it is a symbol so powerful that magical things happen, not only in Strauss's *Rosenkavalier*, but in Théophile Gautier's poem *Spectre de la Rose* which inspired Fokine's ballet for Nijinsky, which became the most popular item in the Diaghilev ballet company's repertoire.

At the more mundane level, by wearing a rose in his buttonhole, a male is signalling to all women that magical things can still happen. In the early years of this century, a special metal rose holder was designed which, filled with water, ensured that the symbol of male sexual power never faded. In the eighteenth and nineteenth centuries the buttonhole in the lapel, which had originally folded across the chest to fasten on a button, closing the male coat at the neck, was commandeered for the flower – usually a rose – which thus itself, in about the 1870s came to be known as the 'buttonhole'.

The moment when Dante met Beatrice, immortalized in his poem, was captured by the little-known Pre-Raphaelite painter Henry Holiday (1839–1927). He is holding a rose in his hand and certainly links Beatrice with the rose in his *Divine Comedy*.

The wild roses in the background were a constant source of trouble to the artist Arthur Hughes, a Pre-Raphaelite whose subject here is the agony of a couple condemned to *The Long Engagement*. The roses closed up when the sun went in and, as a committed Pre-Raphaelite, he had to wait until they came out again before he could begin to paint once more.

There is a certain innocence about the buttonhole rose and love which overcomes the cruder dissonances of its sexual symbolism. For example in *The Young Visiters*, apparently written by an authoress nine years old, when Bernard decides he 'must marry Ethel with no more delay', the following description is given of the proposal scene:

> She looked very beautiful with some red roses in her hat and the dainty red ruge [sic] in her cheeks looked quite the thing. Bernard heaved a sigh and his eyes flashed as he beheld her and Ethel thought to herself what a fine type of manhood he represented with his nice thin legs in pale brown trousers and well fitting spats and a red rose in his buttonhole.

Lovers still use roses as a symbol on cards and other mementoes, as they did in Victorian times. The Valentine card is sometimes decorated with roses.

Entitled 'Two Lovers: The Woman's Dress Caught by the Thorns of a Rose Bush', this pen-and-ink drawing by John Millais (later Sir John) was given to his Pre-Raphaelite 'brother', D.G. Rossetti in 1848. It was intended as an illustration to Thomas Woolner's poem *My Beautiful Lady*, but was never used.

As recently as 1953, a writer in the *Rose Annual* described how the wearing of a buttonhole rose each day between mid-May and early October became his obsession. 'Quite a lot of bushes are needed', he says. 'I cut my buttonholes from about 200 Hybrid Teas, of which over 60 are Standards, the number of varieties being 31'. He claims that he has come to feel that his example has encouraged others into growing where roses did not grow before, and their owners are 'experiencing joys which only rose-growing can bring'. He tells us: 'Picture the scene in a small suburban garden every morning after breakfast. The writer, assisted by his wife, selects a rose with as much if not greater care than he shaves. Let me see, what did I wear on Monday? 'Mme Butterfly'. Yesterday? 'Phyllis Gold'. Then it is the turn of the red.' He has to take account of the problem that it must be in as good a condition for the 7.02 train in the evening as for the 8.03 in the morning. He also admits that when he takes 'a peer in the mirror before leaving for the station, it is not at the face, or the thinning hair, but at the Rose'. He does not like wearing the same variety or even colour, twice in a week.

Today, the buttonhole itself is fading from general use. Most male coats either do not have one or are made with a false buttonhole, with no aperture to take the flower. Tailor-made suits may still enjoy the luxury and the buttonhole remains traditionally essential in the morning suit worn on formal occasions such as weddings, where, however, a carnation in silver foil has replaced the more elegant rose.

The rose retains its popularity as a symbol of the Valentine, originally sent anonymously to the lover but today a commercially boosted ceremony to improve sales in the flat season between Christmas and Easter. It is interesting that while the rose remains the most-bought flower with women, more men buy the carnation.

Indeed the rose itself may in recent years have lost potency as a symbol of love, and its strong connotations of the essence of womanhood. Fewer women are called Rose or Rosie, then they were earlier this century; artists no longer paint the rose with the intensity they once did, not only because of the popularity of abstract rather than representational art, but also because it is perhaps too obvious a symbol. Poets no longer compare their lovers to the rose. Indeed the reverence with which Burns addressed the rose (see the chapter on literature) deteriorated into the following:

> My love is like a red red rose
> Or concerts for the blind,
> She's like a mutton-chop before
> And a rifle-range behind.

This is found in an unpublished typescript poem of five stanzas, 20 lines, undated, by W.H. Auden. Pop stars are unlikely to sing about the last rose of summer. Yet the rose as a plant has never been more popular, and there is some return to the decorative values of the rose-motif in the chintzes and wall-hanging of Laura Ashley and other nostalgia-seeking designers. Is the pendulum swinging back or has the rose as a sex symbol seen its day?

If there has been a disassociation between the rose and romance, we may have to look for the cause not to the rose but to life itself, which has become harsher about the affairs of the heart. Some would describe our attitude to love as more realistic, more matter-of-fact, more diagnostic. After all, it was over 100 years ago that the young writer, Robert Louis Stevenson advised us in one of his essays that 'Marriage is like life in this – that it is a field of battle and not a bed of roses'. As we approach the twenty-first century, it seems that his point of view is generally accepted and a bouquet of roses may no longer be the key to a night of passion.

Rosa picta

VIII

As we approach the twenty-first century, roses are being neglected as a subject for painting. This is clear from relatively conventional collections of art objects such as the Royal Academy's Summer Exhibitions in London, where the rose is already conspicuous by its absence. True, other painterly subjects popular in past times have also virtually disappeared – sailing-boats, cows, angels and saints to name a few – yet somehow the decline of the rose is as surprising as the explanation is hard to find. An easy answer is the development of abstract art, but it is not an answer that satisfies.

The rose has never been a facile subject for the pencil or the brush; failed attempts bear a marked resemblance to a cabbage. In contrast, a really successful rose painter produces an image rich and essentially flower-like, capturing the spirit of the thing in a few brush-strokes that are not in the least photographic. The roses produced by a Renoir or a Fantin-Latour therefore remain powerfully in the memory: surveying the history of art, it is all too easy to believe that the artists of the past were possessed by a kind of rose-fever and that nearly every other painting they produced contained a riot of briers, buds and blossoms.

The same misconception can readily be applied to architecture, where much of church decoration may be recalled as essentially roseate, with cathedrals all over Europe pierced by rose windows. The illusion that the rose dominated art – for illusion it is – has led rose historians to overestimate the influence of the flower itself; a typical claim is that 'contemporary paintings and building decorations make it clear that rose growing from about 1340 to 1700 had become a major activity'. Even if the rose had been a major art object, which it was not, it would not follow that this reflected the scale of rose cultivation.

Art does not always imitate life, nor life art, and painting is probably the least didactic of the arts, except in its religious mode. Something, nevertheless, is needed to account for the erroneous belief that the rose has always been a high-profile subject in art and architecture. One reason may be that from the early Middle Ages the rose was a symbol both for earthly love and for the Virgin Mary's spiritual powers. By the Renaissance, with the revived

PREVIOUS PAGE

Amongst the most famous paintings of roses are the still lifes by the Dutch masters, who uniquely captured in oil paint the dense beauty of such moss roses as this 'Muscosa' – the common moss. They were particularly attracted by the fern-like growths – the 'moss' – which covers the stems and even the long sepals which cover the buds. Moss roses were first mentioned by Elias Peine in his *Hortus Bosianius*. He saw 'Muscosa' in the garden of a senator in Leipzig before 1699.

interest in classical authors, the rose as image of female beauty, of the brevity of love and (to some extent) of sexual passion, also revived. It may be the intensity of these images rather than their universality that gives the impression that the rose was all-pervading in early art.

What did a painting of a rose – or any other powerfully symbolic image – mean to those early painters, and those for whom they painted? Worshippers gazing at the Virgin Mary by the fifteenth-century German master Martin Schongauer (whom Dürer thought great enough to be his own teacher) may well have seen in the roses that surround her an image of the thorny life of sorrow which she must pluck. At about the same period, Stefan Lochner (d. 1451) painted a much more bucolic picture of *The Madonna in a Rose Arbour*. In *The Virgin of the Rosary* by Stefano da Verona, the

The Madonna in this early painting by Stefan Lochner (d. 1451) has a neat little trellis of roses and none of the tragic passion associated with the thorns of the rose.

Nicholas Hilliard (1537–1619), one of the first English miniature painters, excelled at romantic portraits such as this, an anonymous Elizabethan gallant in a rose garden, no doubt about to write a sonnet to his mistress on the brevity of love.

background is a veritable riot of roses, implying that the Virgin was Lady of the Roses. The historian of Marianism, Marina Warner, says that these 'fresh' images of the rose parallel the use of incanting prayers (rosaries) in conjunction with the medieval artefact made of beads, which came to be called the rosary. At the other end of the moral scale, scholars now tell us that Bronzino's *Venus, Cupid, Folly and Time* (*c.* 1540), acquired by Francis I, with Time holding a rose (thought to be *R. chinensis* or Blush China rose) is not a piece of soft porn as we might now think, but a contemporary allegory for venereal diseases. Diane de Poitiers, mistress of Henry II of France, painted at her bath by Clouet, must also have been open-minded about viewers' reaction to the finished portrait, rose and all.

The painting of a *Young Man* by the Elizabethan miniaturist Nicholas Hilliard has a background of simple white roses (*Rosa* x *alba*), indicating not so much the vigour of youth as the brevity of life and 'Time's winged chariot hurrying near'. Many artists of Hilliard's time chose to depict roses because of the qualities they symbolized for their contemporaries, including the poets.

This is not to say that every time a rose is shown it has a hidden meaning, or indeed is even 'art' in our sense of the word. A coin or seal may be a simple artefact with no great artistic merit – as shown on twentieth-century BC Hittite images and the later Assyrian images. It may even be doubted if these are roses at all and not some geometric forms. The same question can be applied even more directly to the image from Crete, dated about 1500 BC. The claim is often made that this is the first rose in art, found at Knossos, Crete, on a wall repainted by Sir Arthur Evans's team of archaeologists.

The first such claim was made by Evans himself. In his *The Palace of Minos*, vol. II, he wrote:

> To the left, for the first time in Ancient Art, appears a wild rose bush, partly against a deep red, and partly against a white background, and other coiling sprays of the same plant hang down from a rockwork arch above. The flowers are of a golden rose colour dotted with deep red. The artist has given the flowers six petals instead of five, and has reduced the leaves to groups of three like those of the strawberry.

Many visitors to Evans's excavations are critical about the extent to which the palace represents the imaginative efforts of Evans and his team. Such suspicions are not put at rest by such remarks as 'the artist has given the flowers six petals instead of five', which beg further questions.

For a time, archaeologists and botanists treated the matter, in Krüssmann's words, as 'a puzzle'. He tells us that the yellow

The famous fresco of the 'Blue Bird' in the Palace of Knossos, Heraklion Museum, Crete, said to have been painted in the sixteenth century BC, is in fact made up from fragments which have been put together by a restorer and, perhaps, overpainted in places by him.

flowers and the bluish-green leaves look like *Rosa persica*, while other botanists were of the view that 'it was a form of *Rosa gallica* artistically altered and simplified'. Another scholar Möbius (1933) thought it was 'probably a rose growing wild in Crete, perhaps *Rosa canina* or *R. dumetorum*'. It is worthwhile to examine the whole subject of Evans's roses a little more closely because it is such a fascinating example of how myths and ascriptions can grow on what may be comparatively little evidence.

Sir Arthur Evans (1851–1941) was a distinguished archaeologist who was also rich enough in his own right to fund the Cretan excavations where he employed not only archaeologists but also craftsmen and artists. The truth about the extent of Evans's 'improvements' at Knossos will never be known. Evans himself was perhaps too preoccupied with the origins of Minoan civilization to be concerned about whether a flower painted on the walls of the palace was the work of an ancient Minoan or a modern improver. Of course, he never admitted to 'improvements'; when he took copies of the frescoes to an Oxford meeting of the British Association in 1926, he was not too precise about which of the flowers were the work of his painting team and which (if any) were by the Minoans.

One of the delegates to the Oxford conference was a young archaeologist and botanist called C.C. Hurst, already one of the most important of English rose researchers, who Evans invited to his house in Oxford to examine the flowers more closely. Hurst was accompanied by his wife Rhona, who later described what happened. What they saw, she said, was not the famous Blue Bird fresco, but probably the one in which there are two monkeys amongst the flowers. She comments that her husband was not unduly perturbed at the colour, nor the fact that the roses had six petals and were trifoliate. After examining the copies, he pronounced them to be 'the earliest depiction of roses known at present'.

Later, in 1941, Hurst wrote a paper for the *Journal of the Royal Horticultural Society* (vol. XLVII) entitled 'Notes on the Origins and Evolution of our Garden Roses' in which he confirmed his view that Evans's rose was an original, not a modern improvement. His paper so impressed the noted rose expert Graham Stuart Thomas that he in turn reprinted it in its entirety in his *Old Shrub Roses* (1955), so giving Evans's rose even more authority.

Rhona Hurst herself, however, was not entirely satisfied, although whether her doubts arose before or after her husband's death is not known. As a botanist of some eminence, as well as an archaeologist, she was well qualified to look at the Knossos roses objectively: she explained how Evans found broken fragments of thin slabs of plaster with the remains of paintings on one side – a major jigsaw puzzle. Pieces found together did not necessarily belong to the same 'puzzle', and often the 'jigsaws' had been painted over when the rooms were redecorated. It was such a muddle that no one fresco remained complete, and Evans had set about the task of completing the puzzle even if this meant sometimes painting some of the pieces.

Mrs Hurst's conclusion was that perhaps one rose of the many now on the frescos was a Minoan painting, and that it bore a marked resemblance to *R. richardii* or to some other form of *R. gallica*. She made the point that this was also the rose found by Petrie in the 1880s, if correctly identified. So far as is known, no other rose expert has been bold enough to enter the lists with an opinion about the provenance of the Knossos rose. Certainly many of those who have seen the frescos and the site will share Mrs Hurst's scepticism about the extent of Evans's 'restoration' and will, in her words, be shocked at the liberties taken. This is not to question the existence of roses in Greece in early times. According to Eva Dierauff, a German rose historian, a clay tablet found in the palace of Nestor at Pylos, dating from 1200 BC, speaks of rose-scented oil.

Many images which may be roses are to be found in later pre-Christian remains. Examples include eighth–ninth century Attic vases, Assyrian vases of around 1000 BC, Etruscan vases of the seventh century BC, rosettes from palaces at Nineveh and Nebuchadnezzar II's palace at Babylon.

In Greek and Roman literature, and to a lesser extent in art, references to roses abound – see for example the rose encircled *Spring* (second century AD) from the Neptune mosaic at Chebra, Tunisia. Many other pagan images of the rose are also to be found in Persia (third–seventh century AD), in northern India (from about the time of the birth of Christ), in Roman Turkey (*c.* AD 130) on Hadrian's Arch. We might question whether any of these images are in fact roses. Might they not be poppies, chrysanthemums or some other flowers? Our uncertainty disappears as soon as the Roman medical writers appear on the scene. For example, there is a drawing which is clearly of a rose, from a copy of Dioscorides' *Materia Medica* dated AD 512. (The book itself was written much earlier, around the time of Christ.) Again, it may be disputed whether botanical illustrations of this kind constitute 'art'.

The truth is that it is not until the fourteenth century that roses are widely used by European painters to add an additional depth of meaning or ambiguity. The same might be said of church architectural decoration. Further east, as we have seen, in Persia and China, the image of the rose appeared earlier still. In the tenth century there are Chinese pictures – botanical drawings we should now call them – of Tea roses and *Rosa rugosa*. *Rosa laevigata* is also illustrated in Ch'iu Huang Peng Ts'ao's *Famine Herbal* of 1406. It is said that this rose (Golden Cherry) was introduced into Europe in the sixteenth century by the East India Company. In Japan, a group of eighth-century poems, *Manyoshu* or *Collection of a Thousand Leaves*, mentions roses and later illustrated versions use the rose to decorate the text.

Persian poets were singing the glories of the rose as early as the ninth century AD and illustrated manuscripts of about this period feature them. They remained a popular subject in Persia until the sixteenth–seventeenth century. As the Muslim religion swept from India to Spain, the rose seems to have travelled with it: the Moors of

Left The Persians, who may well have done more for the development of the rose than any other people, made wide use of it in their decorative art. This section from a door panel, now in the Victoria & Albert Museum, is probably late sixteenth- or early seventeenth-century and was painted for a palace at Isfahan.

Right The rose appears in many fine Persian carpets, and his example, from the Victoria & Albert Museum, is woven in silk tissue in gold and silver.

Morocco were already growing red and white roses in the ninth century. However, it is not until considerably later that the rose appears in their art. Historians tell us that 'blue roses haunted the Moorish mind' – as they do with the modern rose breeder – but they do not appear in their art and it seems doubtful if there were in fact any botanical specimens of pure blue.

In these non-Christian cultures – Chinese, Persian, Muslim – it seems probable that painters of the rose were not attempting religious symbolism. Their roses were nothing more or less than roses. In contrast, the great painters of the early Renaissance, Raphael, Leonardo, Michaelangelo, Botticelli, all employed the rose to add another dimension to the subject of the painting. Similarly woodcuts of the fifteenth century – mostly German – show the Virgin surrounded with roses, which clearly adding a symbolic significance. In 1506, Dürer was commissioned by German merchants working in Venice to paint an idyllic *Festival of the Rose Gardens* (now in the National Gallery, Prague) which shows

Dürer himself, the Emperor Maximilian, Pope Julius II and others offering wreaths of roses to the Virgin. This is an interesting reversal of the *Romaunt of the Rose* theme that the Virgin Mary was the one lady so far above ordinary women as to be able to bestow a rose on her earthly lover.

Renaissance artists sometimes use the rose in paintings which, while they make religious references, are almost secular in intention. An example is Tintoretto's creamy nude Susannah who sits behind a screen of roses which the Elders circumvent in order to study her finer points. Presumably the roses give Susannah respectability, since roses have a strong Marian tradition.

By the time of Poussin, born in the year Tintoretto died (1594), the rose had reverted quite happily to its pagan origins: Poussin's *Bacchanal* has rose-garlanded figures in a riot of naughtiness, kept within the formal arrangement of a classical frieze. In the seventeenth century, the rose was again used to symbolize a short life. Frans Hals painted the immensely rich Haarlem merchant, Willem van Haythusan, full-length, with roses strewn at his feet. In view of the fact that he was a bachelor, the allusion to love is unlikely, and the transience of life the more likely motif. A more direct allusion to love occurs in Hals's pair of portraits, *Stephanus Geraerdts* and *Isabella Coymans* who were married in 1644. Stephanus had chosen wisely as his wife came from one of the wealthiest families in Haarlem. In the left-hand picture of the pair (such portraits always had the lady on the *sinister* side), she proffers a rose as a token of love which he (on the right) puts out a hand to take. Such a device is unique in Hals's work.

The rose as a symbol of earthly love also appears in Boucher's naked girl, now at Munich, some of whose sensual beauty is hidden from us as she lies face down on the couch, with a rose on the floor exactly mirroring the position of her thighs. It is thought the model may have been one of Louis XV's mistresses.

Roses figure heavily in that most popular of paintings, Jean-Honoré Fragonard's *The Swing* of 1786–7. Usually thought to be innocent and charming, things here are not what they seem to be. The picture originated with the desire of a French baron to acquire a representation of his mistress on a swing, with a bishop standing by to add apparent respectability, while the baron himself lay in the grass in a position from which he could observe his mistress's legs as the swing descended. The chosen painter, one Doyen, declined to have anything do with a subject so vulgar. So Fragonard took it on, except that in place of the bishop he put an acquiescent husband giving a helpful hand to the swing of Love. The baron is surrounded by roses symbolizing earthly love.

This picture is not the rustic idyll it appears to be. It was commissioned by a French baron in 1766 who requested that he be shown sitting in the foreground looking at his mistress's legs as the swing rises. Fragonard added the cuckolded husband who enthusiastically pulls the swing from behind. The roses in the foreground are symbolic of the amorous atmosphere.

Fragonard's hero is *Storming the Citadel,* leaping over a wall of roses to reach his objective.

Three or four years later, Fragonard was commissioned by Mme du Barry, Louis XV's mistress, to paint a series of decorative panels for her new pavilions, which would again feature roses. For reasons unknown she returned the panels to the painter in 1773, paying him a hefty sum in compensation, so Fragonard used them to decorate his cousin's house in Grasse. They were finally acquired for the Frick collection in 1915. The first panel, called *Storming the Citadel,* shows the lover leaping over a wall of roses with the assistance of a ladder. The second, *The Pursuit,* shows him offering his mistress a rose, which she rejects in mock shock-horror. By the third panel he has achieved his object and is making *The Declaration of Love* with her in his rosy arms. Panel Four shows *The Lover*

Crowned by his mistress with a garland of roses. This sequence, *The Pursuit of Love*, is an archetypal secularization of the original Virgin Mary myth, right down to the rose garland which she, the most perfect of lovers, can give to her courtly admirer.

Madame du Barry's bed at Versailles was heavily decorated with roses and had a canopy of rose design from which hung silk curtains, also featuring roses. Curtains and furniture were similarly decorated. One of her dresses, which she wore for the wedding of the Comte d'Artois, was described as 'chiné et argent, brodé en papillons verts et roses; les pompons, la palatine et le tour de cou brodé des petites roses'. In the same cultural tradition, though long after the Revolution, Ingres, a painter who pursued the ideal of physical beauty with classical intensity shows his sitter *Madame Moitessier* (1856) as almost a still life dressed in roses. Edouard Manet painted with equal skill, which is perhaps why the salon of 1865 accepted the frankly erotic realism of his *Olympia*, in which the rose plays an important rôle.

Realism was the key to the Pre-Raphaelite Brotherhood's work, and its members were expected to paint roses accurately.

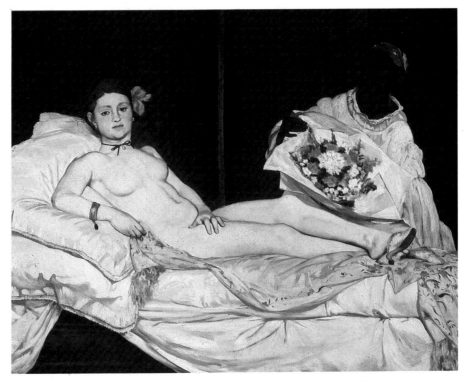

Manet's Olympia accepts a bouquet of roses sent by a lover. The painter's other famous lady, behind the bar at the Folies Bergère, also has rose connections, and Mallarmé called the model for her 'une charmante rose'.

Burne-Jones produced *The Pilgrim and the Rose*, known as his Briar Rose series. It was bought for Buscot Park, Oxfordshire, where it may still be seen today. Another Brother, Arthur Hughes, explains the difficulties he had with his subject *The Long Engagement*, in which two lovers look quite worn out by the experience. 'Painting wild roses . . . has been a kind of match against time with me, they passing away so soon like all the lovely things *under* the sun (eh?) and as sensitive as beautiful. The least hint of rain, just a cloud passing over, closes them up for the day perhaps'.

Fantin-Latour is probably the best-loved of all painters of roses, with a technique far removed from the precision of Redouté. This typical little oil was painted in 1882.

The Empress Eugénie and her maids of honour, by F. X. Winterhalter, *c.*1860, shows how roses and crinolines went so well together. The crinoline seems to say 'keep your distance', while the roses beckon the male admirer.

The Frenchman Henri Fantin-Latour (1836–1904) painted his roses indoors. There may have been a strong element of the feminine in his nature – the first passionate attraction was to the composer Richard Wagner – and his still life of roses have something feminine about them compared with the earlier Dutch masters. Fantin-Latour usually painted *R. gallica*, a rose thought to have its origin in ancient Gaul, and generally believed to be the prototype of such 'old' roses as the Cabbage (*R. centifolia* and its three offspring, the Moss (*R. centifolia muscosa*), Damask (*R. damascena*) and York (*R. x alba*). While there are arguments about this, as about everything else to do with roses, there is no argument though, that Fantin-Latour captured the essential spirit of the rose. Jekyll – no mean painter herself until her eyesight failed – wrote that his 'genius and sympathy enabled him to show on his canvas not only their intrinsic beauty and dignity, but a pathetic suggestion of their relation to human life and happiness'.

The Lady with the Rose produced by Beardsley in 1897, when he was already a dying man.

The most fashionable female dress of Fantin-Latour's time was the crinoline, which the historian James Laver says 'was certainly not a moral garment' – and the rose was frequently selected for its decoration. Winterhalter, a popular painter of the crinoline and the forms that filled it, put the Empress Eugénie in a dress decorated with roses. A few years later, Monet painted his ladies in the garden where it was still fashionable to wear crinolines, perhaps to ward off the pricks of the roses. But before long, although the rose is still in the fashion plates, the crinoline is out, replaced by the tight-laced waisted dress. Even here, roses are used to emphasize the breast, the waist, the bottom and the thighs, as is evident in these plates of 1877. Twenty years later, in the naughty nineties, not much has changed and roses are still used to make a fashionable statement.

If there is a darker side to the rose by the turn of the century, we should expect it in Beardsley's art and indeed it is there in force. There is a rose beside his bare-footed Salomé. Others surround his Venus and Tannhäuser, others are on the gown of his handsome flagellant, on that of Isolde, at the feet of the trans-sexual Pierrot and in the hand of his voluptuous Lady with the Rose. Most beautiful – and enigmatic – of them all is *The Mysterious Rose Garden* which appeared in the *Yellow Book* in 1894. The Art Deco period was also one in which the rose played a significant part – notably in Walter Crane's *Flora's Feast*.

Renoir's passionate affair with roses and the female form has been explored in an earlier chapter. Roses continued to have their place in French art generally – one example is Matisse's *Woman with the Hat*.

If there is something erotic about the rose, one would expect to find it in the work of Aubrey Beardsley. He does not disappoint. Here he offers *Tristan und Isolde*, with another lady, and roses everywhere.

The enigma is that the rose itself is now fading as a subject for artistic endeavour. One reason for this is that photography has taken over from painting where botanical accuracy is required. Redouté remains a popular source for framed pictures for the bedroom, but the colour print has totally ousted botanical engravings for commercial and botanical purposes.

This may be a useful point at which to consider the craft of botanical drawings and paintings. Originally, most plant drawings were, as noted, representational. The woodcuts of the Middle Ages were intended to be so accurate that the cooks and the apothecaries could be clear with which plant they were meddling. The German book *Garden of Good Health* has only one drawing of a rather generalized rose. Hieronymus Bosch's *New Kreutterbuch* (1577) contains 465 woodcuts, although only one is a rose. Matthias Obel from Flanders was court botanist to James I of England; at his garden in Hackney, then a village outside London, he drew some 2173 woodcuts of various plants, of which only ten are roses. Those described and illustrated in his book of 1576 are *R. centifolia, R. gallica, R. canina, R. cinnamomea, R. eglanteria, R. spinosissima, R. foetida* and three forms of *R. moschata*. Gerard's famous *Herball* of 1597 is still reprinted to this day, not so much because of its content as because of its fine illustrations. A year earlier, his *Catalogue Plantarum* illustrated fourteen different roses, all of which probably grew in his garden in Holborn, London.

It is clear how minor a rôle the rose played in these early botanical works. Krüssmann quotes a German herbal which describes 32 tulips, 39 anemones, 44 hyacinths, 60 daffodils, but only 9 roses. In France, the book of Louis XIV's head gardener at Versailles gives details of 77 anemones, 225 carnations, 437 tulips – and 14 roses.

Amongst the most notable of printmakers was Georg Dionysius Ehret (1708–70). His background was horticultural – both his father and his uncle were royal gardeners. In the 1740s he produced a series of watercolours of the classic roses of his time which was so acclaimed that recognition came from noble patrons throughout Europe. Copies of his work are still described today as 'botanical prints', as are Redouté's, although it is questionable whether, whatever the painters' intentions, their work is not more correctly described as art. An English painter who worked at the same time as Redouté was Mary Lawrance. Her *A Collection of Roses from Nature* with 90 hand-coloured etchings appeared in 1799, but is now the rarest of all rare rose books.

Botanical works of the nineteenth and early twentieth centuries have never again reached the standards set by Ehret and Redouté.

The common Provence Rose.

Georg Dionysius Ehret (1708–70) is acknowledged to be one of the finest of rose painters. Born in Heidelberg, Ehret later settled in England and was elected a Fellow of the Royal Society in 1757. One of his patrons was the Duchess of Portland, an ardent botanist, after whom a rose was named.

Though treasured and admired, the paintings of Gertrude Jekyll and Ellen Willmott's protégé, Alfred Parsons RA, are not given the universal admiration awarded to their predecessors.

The borderline between the artist and the craftsman can be studied in museums all over the world. Early embroidery is found with rose motifs, as on a German cape at the Victoria and Albert Museum, delicately worked in gold, silver and coloured silks. By the seventeenth century, almost every craft used roses in some way – fabrics and hangings, leatherwork from Italy and Spain, wooden panelling and furniture. By the eighteenth century, the work had become even more elaborate – table-tops worked in scagliola,

Ellen Willmott (1858–1934) had a considerable influence on rose culture. Between 1910 and 1914 she published her *The Genus Rosa* in parts at her own expense, which bound up into two large volumes. The illustrations were by Alfred Parsons RA whose original watercolours are preserved at the Royal Horticultural Society.

Roses were popular with the Art Nouveau decorative stylists whose work appeared from 1880 until the end of the First World War. Their curling petals complemented curving lines of their models. This candelabrum in ivory and silver is by Egide Rombaux & Franz Hoosemans.

painted tops for chests and bureaux and, of course, carpets. Even the fabrics and papers inspired by Chinese designs featured so-called oriental versions of the rose.

Jewellery fashioned with rose designs has often been worn by the rich, and imitations by the less rich. Cellini made roses in enamel, gold and pearls. Centuries later, Carl Fabergé made some

Claude Monet's *Women in the Garden* are dressed in roses and looking at roses.

of his best pieces in the form of the rose. His biographer, H.C. Bainbridge, said of his work: 'You cannot be funny with flowers. They are the perfection of all created things. Absolute aristocrats, you can't subordinate them: they will do nothing for you except in their own sweet way. . . . You must take no liberties.' What was true for Fabergé is true for all artistic representations of the rose.

It was suggested earlier that the rose's decline in art may have to do with the decline of religion and thus of the Marian myth. Is another contributing factor the decline of the rose itself, not in popularity, but in its essential beauty? One of the most perceptive of modern gardening writers, Robin Lane Fox, calls the average

146

modern rose 'harsh, scentless and garish', while one of the greatest of contemporary British growers, David Austin, says that roses are changing faster now than ever before: 'It is doubtful if the gardeners of earlier times would have been able to immediately recognize many present-day roses as being roses at all.' Austin believes that 'more has been lost than gained. . . . Above all they have lost that essential quality of rosiness'. He continues: 'The rose, it has been assumed, would automatically be beautiful. This unfortunately is not so. There has been a decline in the beauty of Modern Roses . . . [which] are in such harsh shades they do not mix well with other shades. Worse than this they do not mix well with each other.'

Can it be that the artists, 'unacknowledged legislators of the world' (as Shelley called the poets), have already recognized what only a few critics have yet come to see? Gertrude Jekyll, artist as well as garden designer, lived at a time when the colours of garden roses were mainly white, pink, crimson, magenta and purplish – of which her favourites were confined to the cool tints rather than the purples and magentas. 'It should be remembered that a Rose garden can never be called gorgeous,' she wrote. 'The term is quite unfitting. . . . We do not want the mind disturbed or distracted

Picasso's *Three Female Dancers* or *Three Graces* was drawn between 1930 and 1937: they dance with dignity around a pot of roses. The master himself, described as a sculptor, appears to be serene in the face of temptation. Roses rarely appear in modern art, and even 'the great days of botanical art now lie behind us', in the judgement of Wilfred Blunt.

from the beauty and delightfulness of the rose.' She wanted her pastel roses grown in drifts, preferably against a dark green background, and she would have hated the vulgar colours of so many contemporary commercial roses, either for the garden or for 'art'. When we wish to denigrate a painting of roses today we call it 'chocolate box' art. It would be incorrect to suggest that the rose has no place in modern art when it is a subject chosen by painters of such quality as Georgia O'Keefe, whose roses are distinctly symbolic. It is a fading subject in art, nevertheless, and whether the rose can be revived seems doubtful.

Rosa scripta

IX

'What a pother have authors made with Roses!' said Nicholas Culpeper in his *English Herbal Enlarged* of 1653. 'What a Racket they have kept!' We have to remember that by an 'author', Culpeper did not mean the long-haired, artistic variety, with a floppy bow tied at his neck, who was a nineteenth-century invention, but the studious man (there were no women amongst them) who wrote thoughtfully and didactically about the botanical or medical properties of the rose. He was referring to the likes of Bartholomaeus, whose *De Proprietatibus Rerum* (in the 1495 translation) said:

> Among alle flowers of the worlde, the flowre of the rose is cheyf and beeryth ye price [prize]. And therefore ye cheff partyre of man: the heed: is crownyd with flowres of roses, as Plinius sayth. And because of vertues and swete smelle and savour. For by fayrnesse they fede the syghte: and playseth the smelle by odour & touche by nesshe & softe handlynge. And withstandyth & socuryth by vertue ayenst many syknesses & evylles: as he sayth.

John Gerard (1545–1612), surgeon of Holborn, London, grew nine varieties of roses in his garden in 1596 and produced his famous *Herball* in 1597. The illustrations are particularly fine and this probably accounts for the continued popularity of his book.

It was the short-lived nature of the rose that attracted the Renaissance poets who compared it to the brevity of life and love. The greatest poets could give this many a twist. Shakespeare, for

PREVIOUS PAGE

Most poetry and prose about roses describes the wild, simple, once-flowering variety because the writers had never seen hybrids of the type illustrated here, although today we see little else. This, one of the most famous of roses, was introduced in 1958 by the German breeder Reimer Kordes and named 'Schneewittchen' in Europe and 'Iceberg' in England. Kordes was the son of a famous breeder who developed modern field cultivation of roses by budding.

example, in his 54th Sonnet 'Sweet Roses do not so' points out that while other flowers 'die to themselves', roses do not. 'Of their sweet deathes are sweeter odours made'. Similarly, he reasons, his poem will last after his death, and so (he is writing of his patron):

> And so of you, beauteous and lovely youth,
> When that shall fade my verse distils your truth.

Distilling was part of the art of making rosewater. And Shakespeare was aware that his classically educated patron would know that *roseus* was a Latin epithet for anything with the bloom of youth.

It is worth diverging here to comment that in Shakespeare's day the rose was commonly used, just as it is today, as a Christian name, surname, badge of identity, heraldic device, even a commercial brand name. It was not a name apart, with mystic significance. There had been a rose garden on the south side of the Thames in London, in Southwark, and part of the area was therefore called Rose Lane. This was an area of brothels (stews) and at the corner of Rose Lane and Maiden Lane (the latter no doubt an ironic reference to their scarcity in the district), Philip Henslowe had built the Rose Theatre. Lord Strange's Men, led by Edward Alleyn, the greatest tragic actor of the age and Henslowe's son-in-law, opened here in 1592, and the theatre flourished. Near the Rose was the Globe, the Hope and the Swan, as well as a bear garden and a bullring. Later, the Admiral's Men, with whom Shakespeare had connections, played at the Rose. It is indicative of the widespread use of the rose as an image that, according to the concordance, Shakespeare employed the image of the rose some sixty times in his plays.

The rose could be used for sacred as well as profane metaphors. George Herbert, who took holy orders in 1626 (ten years after Shakespeare's death) and published his sacred poems in the following decade, employed the rose as a means of denigrating the world's 'sugred lies' where there is no pleasure. He asks:

> What is fairer than a rose?
> What is sweeter? Yet it purgeth.
> Purgings enmitie disclose,
> Enmitie forbearance urgeth.

> So this flower doth judge and sentence
> Worldly joyes to be a scourge:
> For they all produce repentance
> And repentance is a purge.

> If, then, all that worldlings prize
> Be contracted to a rose;
> Sweetly there indeed it lies,
> But it biteth in the close.

> But I health, not physicke, choose;
> Onely though I you oppose,
> Say that fairly I refuse,
> For my answer is a rose.

A contemporary engraving of the first Rose Theatre on the South Bank, London, in Shakespeare's day.

The rose's short life remained its most significant attribute in the minds of poets of the seventeenth and early eighteenth centuries. Another of Herbert's poems is typical:

> Sweet rose, whose hue angrie and brave
> Bids the rash gazer wipe his eye;
> Thy root is ever in the grave,
>   And thou must die.

Perhaps better-known is Edmund Waller's poem:

> Go lovely Rose –
> Tell her that wastes her time and me,
> That now she knows,
> When I resemble her to thee,
> How sweet and fair she seems to be.
>
> Tell her that's young,
> And shuns to have her graces spied,
> That hadst thou sprung
> In deserts where no men abide,
> Thou must have uncommended died.
>
> Small is the worth
> Of beauty from the light retired:
> Bid her come forth,
> Suffer herself to be desired
> And not blush so to be admired.
>
> Then die – that she
> The common fate of all things rare
> May read in thee;
> How small a part of time they share
> That are so wondrous sweet and fair!

It is sad to think that such a pleasing poem was written by a man who, though a Member of Parliament, is described as time-serving, selfish and cowardly.

The most famous poem of the period is Herrick's, not usually known by its title *To Virgins To Make Much of Time*:

> Gather ye rosebuds while ye may,
> Old time is still a-flying:
> And this same flower that smiles today
> Tomorrow will be dying.

Herrick took holy orders and was appointed to a small parish in Devon, which seems a far remove from the sentiments of this most pagan of his poems. He was certainly typical of seventeenth-century poets in bemoaning the rose as a symbol of lost time (remember that they did not know a rose which was able to repeat-flower until the arrival of the China rose.)

In the following century, poets do not appear to have much time for the rose. One exception is Burns, and his use of the rose symbol is brief and to the point.

> O, my Luve's like a red, red rose
> That's newly sprung in June.
> O, my Luve's like the melodie
> That's sweetly played in tune.

Here it is only necessary for Burns to use the word 'rose' for the appropriate romantic response to be sprung. Much the same might be said of that other great lyricist Thomas Moore who sang

> Tis the last rose of summer
> Left blooming alone
> All her lovely companions
> Are faded and gone.

The sentiment dates the piece – the modern rose goes on well into the autumn.

William Blake was an eighteenth-century poet and also one of the first of the romantics. Alternatively, he can be categorized as a member of no movement, rather a native, an original. His poem on the rose is typical Blake, since there is nothing like it in the rest of literature. Perhaps it is because it is so curious that it is mentioned neither in the *Oxford Book of English Verse* (first edition) nor in the *Oxford Dictionary of Quotations*. No doubt the reason is that the editors were puzzled as to its meaning, and rightly so. It reads as follows:

THE SICK ROSE

> O Rose, thou art sick: Has found out thy bed
> The invisible worm   Of crimson joy;
> That flies in the night,   And his dark secret love
> In the howling storm,   Does thy life destroy.

The Love of Roses

This was one of Blake's *Songs of Experience* of 1794, the same volume which contained the famous poem *Tyger, Tyger, Burning Bright*. (There is no original copy of the *Songs of Experience* as a separate publication: it appeared in one volume called *The Songs of Innocence and Experience Showing the Two Contrary States of the Human Soul*.) His biographer, Mona Wilson, explains that in the *Songs of Innocence,* published as a single volume in 1789, Blake had revealed the innocence of the mystic, but later, like all mystics, he was overwhelmed with self-disgust. 'He had looked on the world through the eyes of a child: he must now see it through the eyes of a man who perceives all the evil and misery, and rebels against the errors which cause them . . . . Some critics are surprised that 'The Lilly', which opposes innocence and experience in a single quatrain, was not included among the *Songs of Innocence,* but the irony of the adjectives 'modest' and 'humble' seems to have escaped them.' That poem also refers to the rose:

> The modest Rose puts forth a Thorn,
> The humble Sheep a threat'ning horn,
> While the Lilly White shall in Love delight,
> Nor a thorn nor a threat stain her beauty bright.

It is clear that Blake found the rose a powerful symbol of evil as well as beauty. In another poem in the *Songs of Experience* he is just as specific.

My Pretty ROSE TREE

> A FLOWER was offer'd to me,
> Such a flower as May never bore;
> But I said 'I've a Pretty Rose-tree'
> And I passed the sweet flower o'er.
>
> Then I went to my Pretty Rose-tree
> To tend her by day and by night;
> But my Rose turned away with jealousy,
> And her thorns were my only delight.

Blake is taking us deeper into human experience than the *carpe diem* poets of the previous century. They merely used the rose as a means of reflecting on the brevity of life and love. In contrast, Blake describes the rose as both beautiful and evil. Of all the poems in the English language that use the rose as a symbol, his are perhaps the most profound. Gardeners who believe that the rose is the most beautiful of all nature's flowers might well contemplate Blake's poems, and ask themselves if life is not concerned with other aspects of experience than beauty. They may have exorcized his insights by encouraging the breeders to produce thornless roses, but in doing so they have over-simplified the message of nature which, according to Blake, is more complex than the innocent's idea of beauty.

Young John Keats, the most romantic of the Romantic poets, naturally preferred the wild rose to what he called 'the garden-rose', which by his time (1795–1821) had become much cultivated. He wrote the following in 1816 when he was studying at Guy's Hospital:

> I saw the sweetest flower wild nature yields,
> A fresh blown musk-rose 'twas the first that threw
> Its sweets upon the summer; graceful it grew
> As is the wand that Queen Titania wields
> And, as I feasted on its fragrancy
> I thought the garden-rose it much excelled.

This is in the sonnet 'To A Friend Who sent me some Roses' and the concluding lines tell us that the friend concerned was Charles Wells.

> But when, O Wells! thy roses came to me,
> My sense with their deliciousness was spell'd:
> Soft voices had they, that with tender plea,
> Whispered of peace, and truth, and friendliness unquell'd

The irony is that Wells, then a bouncing red-haired youth of seventeen and a school-friend of Keats's brother Tom, was over-fond of practical jokes and may have sent the roses either as a jape or as an apology after offending Keats (see Keats's reference to 'friendliness unquell'd'). Two or three months later, Wells set up an elaborate practical joke by sending Tom letters purporting to be from a girl in love with him. After Tom's death in 1818, however, Keats discovered the letters amongst his brother's papers, spotted the deception, and, believing that the prank had contributed to the decline in Tom's health, acrimoniously broke off his friendship with the bumptious Wells.

Amongst the most quoted lines of poetry on a rose theme are those taken from Edward Fitzgerald's translation of Omar Khayyám's *Rubáiyát*. Omar Khayyám was a Persian astronomer and mystic, while Fitzgerald was a gentleman and dilettante from Suffolk. The latter translated *The Rubáiyát* from the Persian when he was about fifty years old, but the poem, when published, fell with a deafening thud upon the mid-Victorian reading public. Fortunately for Fitzgerald (who had printed the poem at his own expense and anonymously), the publisher Quaritch put the despised book in a 'penny box' outside his shop, where it was discovered by friends of the poet and painter Rossetti, who in turn showed it to his friend Swinburne. The latter gives this account of what happened:

A fifteenth-century Persian prince in a rose-patterned robe. Persia may have been the home of the rose, from where it spread to Greece, Rome and further west.

Having read it, Rossetti and I invested upwards of sixpence apiece – or possibly threepence – I would not wish to exaggerate our extravagence – in copies at that not exorbitant price. Next day we thought we might get some for presents amongst friends – but the man at the stall asked twopence! Rossetti expostulated with him in terms of such humourously indignant remonstrance as none but he could ever have commanded. We took a few, and left him. In a week or two, if I am not mistaken, the remaining copies were sold at a guinea; I have since – as I dare say you have – seen copies offered for still more absurd prices.

Fitzgerald remodelled and enlarged *The Rubáiyát* in 1868, and changed his mind again in 1872 and 1879, when he reduced its length, but by this time it had become one of the most popular poems in the language and Fitzgerald one of the most famous of poets. His fame rests on this one poem, and a curious sort of fame it is, since the meaning of the poem is frequently obscure and, where the meaning is clear, somewhat banal. The references to the rose suffer from both these disadvantages.

Tradition has it that Omar not only chose the site of his grave, but also desired that roses should be planted on it, while he himself is to be 'in a winding sheet of vine leaf wrapt'. The message for those who remain alive is that:

> While the Rose blows along the River Brink
> With old Khayyam the Ruby Vintage drink;
> And when the Angel with his Darker draught
> Draws up to thee – take that and do not shrink . . .

An article in the *Rose Annual* (1950) by a Mr F. P. Knight says that the old bush in Boulge churchyard near Woodbridge, where Fitzgerald was buried, had almost certainly died, but some members of the Omar Khayyám Club (or Omarians as they are sometimes called) succeeded in gathering a few buds 'at the last moment' and grafting them on to stocks of *R. rugosa* from which healthy plants were raised in Notcutt's nursery at Woodbridge in

The poet Omar Khayyám made much of roses, at least in the translation by Edward Fitzgerald, and it is fitting that the latter's tomb in a Suffolk churchyard should have been decorated with the Damask roses from the Persian poet's tomb. Over the years the grave has been neglected, but a new bed of roses was planted by admirers in recent years.

1949. Mr Knight wrote this from Woodbridge, so it is no doubt reliable intelligence.

Meanwhile Kew had concentrated on raising a new plant from the old one at Kew and this was sent to Boulge churchyard too. When Mr Knight had last visited the grave it 'appeared to have become established'.

René Bull illustrated a modern version of the Omar Khayyám, this picture being captioned 'Ah Love!', an aspect of the poem which has appealed to many readers.

The nearer we come to the present day, the more it seems that the literary rose loses specificity of image and becomes a vague symbol of beauty. One well-known Swinburne line is about the change of 'The lilies and langours of virtue/For the raptures and roses of vice.' A rather fuller version is given in his poem

> Forth, ballad, and take roses in both arms,
> Even till the top rose touch thee in the throat.
> Where the least thorn-prick harms;
> And girdled in thy golden singing coat
> Come thou before my lady and say this:
> Borgia, thy hair's gold colour burns in me,
> Thy mouth makes beat my blood in feverish rhymes,
> Therefore so many as these roses be,
> Kiss me so many times.

This is not far from the kind of thing that the writer of a sentimental song might say about roses. The same might be felt about Tennyson and his 'Queen rose of the rosebud garden of girls' from *Maud* about whom the red rose cried 'She is near, she is near/And the white rose weeps, "She is late."' This was after 'The lillies and roses were all awake/They sigh'd for the dawn and thee'.

A similarly banal view of the rose is taken by Walter Crane in his *Flora's Feast, A Masque of Flowers*. Crane (1845–1915) became Principal of the Royal College of Art in London, and was a follower of the socialist views of William Morris, though there is nothing revolutionary about his attitude to the rose.

When Swinburne was in his middle forties, a young admirer of his, then aged only 16, produced the following rather sophisticated poem, entitled '*Roses*':

> Roses by babies' rosier fingers pressed
> In wondering amazement. Later, youth
> Attired in knickbockers, flings them by
> Contemptuously. Lover's openings then,
> Much kissed and withered. Staid and sober age
> In snug, suburban villas rears them last:
> The world at large is dowered with their thorns!

Kipling (for it was he), in staid and sober age, became just such a gardener as he describes, although he would not have described his Sussex house, Bateman's, as suburban. His poem about gardening, *The Glory of the Garden* (1911) has become one of the most popular anthology pieces on the subject.

An exact contemporary of Kipling, but a very different kind of poet, W. B. Yeats, was one of the last great poets in the English language to use the rose as a symbol with neither sentimentality nor

Lewis Carroll's *Alice in Wonderland*, like the *Roman de la Rose*, a dream in which the rose plays a part. The tyrannical Queen of Hearts wants red roses: Alice finds the gardeners changing the white ones with pots of paint to meet the royal command.

self-consciousness. Yeats's collection *The Rose,* published in 1893, contains many of his finest and best-known poems, many written before he was twenty years old. *The Lake of Innisfree, When you are old,* and *The Man who dreamed of Faeryland* are among them. The opening poem, called *To The Rose upon the Rood of Time,* begins:

> Red Rose, proud Rose, and Rose of all my days!
> Come near me, while I sing thy ancient ways.

What did the rose mean to Yeats? A few years later, when he was publishing his next collection, the poet explained: 'The Rose is a favourite symbol with Irish poets . . . a symbol of spiritual love and supreme beauty'. In *The Secret Rose,* written in 1899, the spiritual seems uppermost in his mind. Here is the opening and the conclusion:

> Far-off, most secret, and inviolate Rose
> Enfold me in my hour of hours; where those
> Who sought thee in the Holy Sepulchre,
> Or in the wine-vat, dwell beyond the stir
> And tumult of defeated dreams; and deep
> Among pale eyelids, heavy with the sleep
> Men have named beauty . . .
>
> Surely thine hour has come, thy great wind blows,
> Far-off, most secret, and inviolate Rose?

Another poem, written about the same time, dwells on the beauty of the rose and is one of the most famous poems he wrote. It is *The Lover tells of the Rose in his Heart.* In it, Yeats laments

> All things uncomely and broken, all things worn out and old,
> The cry of a child by the roadway, the creak of a lumbering court,
> The heavy steps of the ploughman, splashing the wintry mould,
> Are wronging your image that blossoms a rose in the deeps of my
>   heart.

Burne-Jones, a prominant member of the Pre-Raphaelite Brotherhood, designed this tapestry called *The Pilgrim and the Rose* (1901), which no doubt harks back to the *Romaunt of the Rose*, a product of the medieval age which he idolized.

The wrong of unshapely things is a wrong too great to be told;
I hunger to build them anew and sit on a green knoll apart,
With the earth and the sky and the water, remade, like a casket of
   gold
For my dreams of your image that blossoms, a rose in the deeps of
   my heart.

Yeats wrote that he imagined 'the quality symbolised as the Rose' as 'suffering with man and not wholly pursued and seen from afar'. As with many poets, the thorns of the rose were as present in his mind as its blossoms. This was particularly true when, after the Irish Easter Uprising of 1916, Yeats came to write about the men who deliberately gave their lives in the belief that by so doing they would change Irish politics. Foremost among them was Pearse. In his poem about the withered rose tree, Yeats has Pearse say to Connolly:

O Plain as plain can be
There's nothing but our own red blood
Can make right a Rose Tree.

Already younger poets were using somewhat 'unpoetical' imagery by nineteenth-century standards. One of them, Rupert Brooke, thought to be more of a traditionalist than he really was, wrote in his best-known poem *The Old Vicarage, Grantchester* (written in a Berlin café in 1912):

> *Temperamentvoll* German Jews
> Drink beer around; and *there* [i.e. Grantchester] the dews
> Are soft beneath a morn of gold.
> Here tulips bloom as they are told;
> Unkempt about those hedges blows
> An English unofficial rose;

There had to come a time when someone would look at the rose afresh in literary or poetic terms. It came in the person of the strange, dumpy American in Paris, Gertrude Stein, who wrote the famous line, quoted here in her poem *I am a Rose* (part of *Sacred Emily*),

> A rose is a rose is a rose
> I am a Rose my eyes are blue
> I am a Rose and who are you
> I am a Rose and when I sing
> I am a Rose like anything

(She later wrote the first and famous line in a circle to show that even when spoken an infinite number of times it still made no more sense.) This, when published in 1934, was a profound shock even to those who agreed with Shakespeare's 'What's in a name? That which we call a rose/By any other name would smell as sweet'. Exactly what Stein meant by it remained unclear until, when she was 61 years old, she was lecturing to a class of young students in Chicago. One of them asked her the meaning of 'A rose is a rose is a rose' (it must have taken some courage). Her reply was:

> Now listen. Can't you see that when language was new – as it was with Chaucer and Homer – the poet could use the name of a thing and the thing was really there. He could say 'O moon', 'O sea', 'O love' and the moon and the sea and love were really there. And can't you see that after hundreds of years had gone by and thousands of poems had been written, he could call on those words and find that they were now wornout literary words. The excitingness of pure being had withdrawn from them; they were just rather stale literary words. Now the poet has to work in the excitingness of pure being; he has to get back that intensity into the language. We all know that it's hard to write poetry in late age; and we know that you have to put some strangeness, as something unexpected, into the structure of the sentence in order to bring back vitality to the noun. Now

it's not enough to be bizarre; the strangeness in the sentence structure has to come from the poetic gift itself. That's why it's doubly hard to be a poet in a late age. Now you all have seen hundreds of poems about roses and you know in your bones that the rose is not there. All those songs that sopranos sing about 'I have a garden! Oh, what a garden!' Now I don't want to put too much emphasis on that line because it's just one line in a long poem. But I notice that you all know it; you make fun of it, but you all know it. Now listen! I'm no fool. I know that in daily life we do not go around saying ' . . . is a . . . is a . . . is a . . .'. Yes, I'm no fool but I think that in that line the rose is red for the first time in English writing for a hundred years.

T. S. Eliot may have been fond of roses – we are told he used to send them to ladies to whom he was attached. It would certainly have taken a brave student to have asked such a distinguished poet whether the rose meant anything more to him than just the conventional romantic symbol. In the *Four Quartets*, over which he laboured long and hard in the years of the Second World War, the references to the rose include 'dust on a bowl of rose-leaves'; 'late roses filled with early snow'; 'frigid purgatorial fires of which the flame is roses, and the smoke is briars'; and 'a door we never opened into the rose garden'.

In a section of the poem dealing with 'love of country', Eliot says that celebrating dead men is *'not to ring the bell backward/Nor is it*

Gertrude Stein, the author and art patron, was responsible for one of the most crushing criticisms of rose culture when she wrote 'A rose is a rose is a rose'. This portrait by Picasso, her friend and protégé, was painted in 1906.

an incantation/To summon the spectre of a Rose.' Eliot's most famous mention of the rose appears in the last line of the poem in the section *Little Gidding.* (George Herbert had been influenced by the seventeenth-century parson of Little Gidding.) He has been discussing throughout how 'the end of all our exploring/Will be to arrive where we started/And know the place for the first time' and concludes that we should acquire

> A condition of complete simplicity
> (Costing not less than everything)
> And all shall be well
> And all manner of thing shall be well
> When the tongues of flame are infolded
> Into the crowned knot of fire
> And the fire and the rose are one.

What does he mean? Eliot became irritated when anyone asked what his poetry meant and was inclined to snap either that it meant what it said, or that it was no use asking him.

Some clue may be found in his *Ash Wednesday* of 1930, written when he had abandoned his family's Unitarian faith. It was an attempt, in his own words, to apply Dante's *Vita Nuova* to contemporary life. He wrote:

> Rose of memory
> Rose of forgetfulness
> Exhausted and life-giving
> Worried reposeful
> The single Rose
> Is now the Garden
> Where all loves end
> Terminate torment
> Of love unsatisfied
> The greater torment
> Of love satisfied

By the time he wrote the *Four Quartets* in 1942, Eliot saw the earlier tradition of Dante 'shimmering like an hallucination before it disappears and the sirens of a catastrophic European war intrude'. So the rose is a symbol of the past, with powerful religious connotations, about to be consumed into the flame, creating by fire a new life into which the rose is absorbed rather than destroyed. If such an 'explanation' of the later poem's meaning is even half correct, Eliot is signalling the death of the rose as a symbol in its own right.

To suggest that the rose has altogether disappeared as a poetical image of love, death and decay would be going too far. It is still called forth – for example, by Sylvia Plath writing about a plaster cast of her head in 1961:

> Without me, she wouldn't exist, so of course she was grateful.
> I gave her a soul. I bloomed out of her as a rose
> Blooms out of a vase of not very valuable porcelain.

It has to be said that this is not one of Plath's most powerful poems.

The emphasis in this chapter has been on the rose in poetry or in lyrical song. Plenty of prose was also spent on roses but it was, as Culpeper noted, the prose of descriptive writers explaining the utilitarian rose: herbal, medicinal, culinary and so on. When it comes to what we should nowadays call creative prose, the rose does not get much of a look in. We would not expect Jane Austen to have much time for the rose, nor George Eliot, and certainly not Sir Walter Scott, although it was he who invented the term *The Wars of the Roses* to describe the military campaigns between the Houses of York and Lancaster.

No novelist of note in the nineteenth century, when the novel was at the height of its popularity, used the rose as a major theme. It is the kind of image that might have appealed to Henry James, to whom a golden bowl or a figure in a carpet had particular significance, but apparently it did not. The only notable writer to seize upon the rose was Oscar Wilde, in a rare story. Wilde, the dandy, is remembered for wearing a green carnation in his buttonhole, and perhaps he did so because it was easier to dye a carnation than a rose. His tale of the rose invests it with considerable significance. It is called *The Nightingale and the Rose*. Wilde relates how a young student has a sweetheart who tells him that she will only dance with him if he brings her a red rose. He

Drawing of a Persian embroidery of the early seventeenth century from Isfahan, representing (left) *R. foetida* and (right) 'Persian Yellow' with nightingales and a deer. The nightingale is often associated with the rose, notably by Oscar Wilde. Isfahan, sometimes called the Persian City of Roses, still has roses in its streets and parks today.

can find none in his garden. As he bewails his fate, a nightingale takes pity on him and offers to help him find one amongst the yellow and white roses with which the garden is filled. The nightingale finds a red bush but all its blooms have been killed by frost. In desperation, the nightingale cries: 'One red rose is all I want – only one red rose. Is there no way by which I can get it?' 'There is a way,' the rose tree replies, 'but it is so terrible that I dare not tell it to you.' 'Tell it to me,' says the nightingale. 'I am not afraid.' 'If you want a red rose,' says the tree, 'you must build it out of music by moonlight, and stain it with your own heart's blood. You must sing to me with your breast against a thorn. All night long you must sing to me and flow into my veins and become mine.' The nightingale decides that 'Love is better than life' and sacrifices her life to bring the love-sick student his rose. (Note that the nightingale is feminine.) When the student gives the rose to his lover, she says that she prefers jewels and throws the bloom angrily away. This typically Wildean and somewhat sadistic story is of course based on the Persian myth of the nightingale.

Wilde was a poet manquée, who made his living as a dramatist and story-teller because it was amusing to do so, and because it was more lucrative than poetry. The rose is not the stuff of prose.

The rose is, nowadays, not the subject of literature either. Perhaps this is because the rose itself is changing, forced by the commercial demands of the horticultural trade to be something that it never was. The American essayist Emerson could not, with hindsight, have been more wrong than when he wrote:

> An everlasting NOW reigns in nature, which hangs the same roses on our bushes which charmed the Roman and the Chaldean in the hanging gardens.

Alas we must also recall that Emerson said that 'money is as beautiful in its operations and effects as roses'. Some modern commercial rose growers may have been quoting this to themselves as they selected this year's new model, garish, scentless, disease-free, and very marketable.

$\overline{\text{X}}$

Rosa utilis

Just before Christmas in 1989, shoppers at Harrods in Knightsbridge, London, found amongst the many goodies on offer some of the most expensive soap ever made. Gloriously set in a packing which resembled a leather-bound book, two bars were being offered for £150. A numbered limited edition of only 500 of these packs was available to the discriminating and, apart from their price, the quality which made them irresistible was their exquisite perfume. While redolent of a traditional rose fragrance it was different in a subtle way. The reason for this olfactory distinction was that the essential rose oil it contained had been extracted from rose petals by the inventive Yorkshire microbiologist Dr Peter Wilde, using a unique process which he had pioneered and which had permitted his company, Floral Fragrances of Thirsk in Yorkshire, to become the first organization in Britain for two centuries to begin extracting rose oil commercially.

Wilde's rose-scented soap appealed to Harrods' shoppers.

Wilde sought the essence of the rose.

In that first year of operation, Wilde grew too few roses to produce more than a litre of the essential oil and so he decided to have it made into a limited quality of 'up-market' soap. Its ready acceptance as a luxury item confirmed his belief that there was a market for a high-quality rose oil of the type which he could make and this compensated him for his previous disappointments. For the story of his entry into the rose oil supply business is likely to

---

PREVIOUS PAGE

'Trigintipetala' is a Damask rose grown in quantity for its oil in the Balkans and Russia. It is known in Bulgaria as 'Rose of Kazanlik' because of its commercial importance as attar of roses from that area.

The Indian Princess Nur-mahal and her husband, the Great Moghul. According to legend it was she who first discovered a method of obtaining Attar. Krüssmann says that Attar is basically an Arabic word which means 'scent'. It is derived from *a'thara* which means anything with a pleasant smell. Therefore, in the orient, the words *Athar Gul* stand for oil of roses, and *gulab* is rose-water.

become an often repeated commercial saga. Some years ago, dissatisfied with the concentrated liquid coffee extracts which were available, he developed something better. It was so superior to other coffee concentrates that he found no difficulty in selling his process very profitably to a Belgian firm which sold coffee in large quantities to caterers.

But like most inventors, Wilde, who had already gained an international reputation in the engineering field following the invention of a novel hose clip which has been very widely adopted, was never completely happy with his achievement. 'I knew that my new coffee concentrate was good,' he explained. 'But it was never as good as was promised by the wonderful fragrance I had enjoyed in the laboratory. In fact I realized that coffee is hardly ever as good as it smells and I decided to find out why.'

He knew, from the result of early experiments, that the ethereal oils responsible for the aroma of coffee were only present in minute quantities and that they boiled off at relatively low temperatures. So although the kitchen might smell wonderful, there was very little of the oil responsible for coffee's enticing fragrance (and probably its most appealing element) left by the time it had reached the cup.

Making his concentrated coffee extract had involved high temperatures and inevitably a lot of the fugitive oils had been lost. Wilde made many attempts to improve the process, and ultimately succeeded triumphantly by extracting all the vital ingredients in a solvent which has such a low boiling point that it is only liquid at minus 40 degrees centigrade. This chilly extraction process yielded a product with a much higher than normal content of the ethereal oils, but it was quite costly because it had to take place in very sophisticated low-temperature apparatus. Nevertheless, Wilde felt that the great expense of the apparatus would be more than justified by the superiority of the product on the market. He therefore decided to offer the new process to his former clients.

Instead of the grateful reception which he had anticipated, they said that they were perfectly satisfied with the process which he had previously developed for them. Since the company was one of the major catering coffee suppliers, Peter Wilde, in his own words, found himself 'with a wonderful process and nothing to make with it'. On reflection, he realized that his process might be applicable to the extraction of lavender oil or rose oil and, realizing that lavender oil was already being produced in commercial quantities in Britain, he elected to investigate the extraction of rose oil. His first step was to visit Turkey to discover how that job was tackled there. He chose Turkey because, with 18,000 acres of roses grown for oil production, it was a major producer. Other less accessible areas of production were Bulgaria, with 40 square miles devoted to the crop, and Russia which claims to grow even more.

The notion of extracting rose oil also appealed to Peter Wilde because he was aware of what he thought was a very sad story. It

The ancient British tradition of anointing the monarch (here Edward VII) with rose-water.

appears that from the time of Elizabeth I every British sovereign had been anointed at their coronation with a 'holy oil' containing rose oil of British origin. In 1952, however, when the 'holy oil' was needed for the coronation of Queen Elizabeth II, it was found that the flask had been broken when Westminster Abbey was damaged during the war blitz. A new flask was made for the coronation and filled with a 'holy oil' containing rose oil of either Bulgarian or Turkish origin. If such alien rose oil is used to anoint future British monarchs, Peter Wilde will be sadly disappointed. According to a recent biography, Prince Charles is already growing strongly-scented roses in order to make an essence. Dr Wilde suggested that the heir to the throne should process his own essential oils, and the process of extraction has already begun. The primary object is to produce enough oil for aromatherapy, a type of massage enjoyed by both the Prince and his wife, but its use in the Coronation service is also in mind. Dr Wilde wittily observes: 'If the Prince does follow through this scheme to make his own "holy oil", it would be do-it-yourself on a truly majestic scale.'

In Turkey and Bulgaria the rose oil is extracted from *Rosa damascena* 'Trigintipetala'. The processors use the traditional steam extraction technique, mixing half a tonne of freshly picked flower heads with one-and-a-half tonnes of water in a still. The first half tonne of water is boiled off as steam and condensed. The top layer of the condensate is the attar or rose oil which floats on the pleasingly lightly rose-scented water of condensation which is called rosewater. The oil extracted in this process is initially called 'Concrete' and contains many undesirable contaminants. It is refined to a state known as 'Absolute' when absolute alcohol, which has been shaken with the concrete to dissolve out the rose oil, is distilled off to yield the pure oil. Approximately two tonnes of rose petals will yield only one kilogram of essential oil, one reason why for centuries this product has been so highly prized. And despite large-scale production of the oil it still attracts prices of up to £4000 per kilogram for a high-quality sample.

It was undoubtedly the considerable value of the product which had tempted a gardener, James Potter, and his uncle, an apothecary, James Moore, to found their rose oil extraction business at Figs Marsh in Upper Mitcham near London in 1790. At its height their company was so successful that it was growing 350 acres of plants for extraction and operating five stills. However, the cost of hand labour necessary to harvest the roses just as their petals are beginning to open fully made it inevitable that producers in Britain could not compete with oil from the Balkans with its peasant economy. Potter & Moore were the first British entrepre-

Bulgarian ladies celebrate the gathering of rose petals.

neurs to attempt a rose oil business on a substantial scale; after their failure it seemed they would also be the last.

Uninhibited by traditional attitudes in the rose oil extraction industry, Peter Wilde had already carried out trials on 140 varieties to determine the suitability of many modern hybrid roses both as a raw material and as crop plants in his area of Yorkshire. 'Gertrude Jekyll', for example, one of the more fragrant results of the breeding programme by David Austin of Wolverhampton, has proved to be a much more efficient producer of rose oil than *Rosa damascena*, and it has the great advantage of blooming for a much longer period. This means that by growing a series of different roses which tend to produce their blooms sequentially throughout the summer, Wilde will be able to run his extraction equipment for much longer each season. And whereas traditional processing still leaves the petals as a wet mush and in a state only fit to be used as compost, Wilde's process leaves them dry and quite unblemished so that they could be used as a base for pot pourri or other products such as rose-petal pillows.

The only limit to the expansion of his business is the availability of a large enough local supply of the ten varieties of rose he considers the most useful. They must be grown locally because from the moment the blooms are picked they begin to deteriorate rapidly, so that to obtain the best yields of oil the roses must be processed as soon as possible. So far, several local farmers have agreed to produce roses for him. In return, adopting a microbiological approach, he has arranged to have thousands of young roses produced by micropropagation in laboratories in Darwin, Australia, which should be coming into production in the 1990 season.

Because they contain ingredients which were not present in rose oils extracted by traditional methods, cosmetic and perfumery products perfumed with Peter Wilde's rose oil have a different fragrance to any previous products, and he can genuinely claim to have advanced the perfumier's art. And as far as the extraction of rose oil is concerned, he has made the first major advance in 600 years. For it was in the fourteenth century that it was first discovered that essential oils could be extracted from flower petals by dissolving them in alcohol. Prior to that, the distillation of the petals mixed with water was the usual extraction process. This technique is said to have been developed by Avicenna, an Arabian doctor, in the tenth century.

By the fifteenth century, few large homes or monastery hospitals were without equipment to distil roses and other flowers, and sectors of the garden were set aside to produce blooms for that purpose. Before the introduction of distillation, other techniques

The little 'Gertrude Jekyll' rose, named after the famous Edwardian gardener, was bred by David Austin. It has proved to be not only highly fragrant but an efficient producer of rose oil.

173

were used to extract the perfume from roses. One of them, employed by the Romans, was to dissolve out the wax and essential oil by mixing the petals with olive oil to form an unguent body rub which was called stymata. This rather slower and less efficient process works because the essential oil of roses contains at least eight major ingredients, among them geraniol, which are present in specialized storage cells on the upper surface of the petal. While in those cells, the oils are in an inert form mixed with a sugar to form a glucoside which only breaks down into the more volatile oil liberated as a scent when the flower buds open and the top of the petals is exposed to the air and oxidation has taken place. As the scent escapes from the storage cells, it is replaced by further glucoside from adjacent cells in the epithelium of the petal. The extraordinary pungency of these essential oils is demonstrated by the fact that it is often possible on fairly still days to detect the scent of a single rose many yards downwind, when only minute qualities of the oil can be evaporating from the small area of exposed petal surface. However, that they can be detected at all is due to the extreme sensitivity of man's sense of smell. As Roy Genders pointed out in his book *Scented Flora of the World*, 'whereas the gas chromatographic which is one of the most sensitive pieces of laboratory analytical equipment can detect as little as a thousandth of a millionth of a gramme of certain substances, the human nose can detect one hundreth of that'.

According to herb expert, Sarah Garland, it was red and pink roses – *Rosa damascena, Rosa gallica* (the Provins or apothecary's rose) and the fragrant Cabbage roses – which were traditionally used to make pot pourri. The term 'rotten pot' for this ancient product which was used to sweeten the air derives from one method of production that allowed layers of moist petals to rot down in a pot to form an 'aromatic cake'.

In practice, batches of three pints of rose petals, one pint each of peony petals, clove carnation petals and sweet marjoram petals and leaves, plus half a pint of lavender flowers, myrtle leaves and

Rosa damascena; from de l'Obel's *Kruydtboeck* (1581).

lemon verbena leaves, after partial drying for two days, should be laid in a large pot, sprinkled with a handful of rock salt and weighed down with a heavy plate. Before further smaller layers are added to the mass as the summer progresses, the mixture should be stirred. Stirring should be repeated before adding another layer of salt when the pot is virtually full. Then it should be left weighed down for a further fortnight by which time it should have formed a cake. Eight tablespoons of brandy, two of brown sugar, the dried and powdered rinds of an orange and a lemon, plus eight dried bay leaves, and ½ oz each of grated nutmeg, powdered cloves, orris and allspice should be thoroughly mixed with the fragmented cake before being weighted down in the pot again, where it should spend six months maturing.

Such a mixture was traditionally kept in a closed vessel which was warmed and then opened to liberate its scent when required. Rose petals, too, have long been used to make a dry but equally complicated version of *pot pourri*, in which the individual ingredients are fully dried before being mixed.

Apart from their use as raw material for extracting oil and making rosewater, roses have also been used as a base for incense which could be used to sweeten the air. A recipe from 1662 suggests using ¼ pint rosewater (to which a tablespoon of powdered clove has been added) dropped into a hot pan.

It was more than just the desire to release the pleasing fragrance of rose oil – as it usually is today – which motivated the use of roses as something more than perfumes or cosmetics. Smelly and insanitary places were associated with disease (often correctly) long before Louis Pasteur had taught us about the infective capacity of micro-organisms. Freshening the air with light perfume, or in extreme cases fumigating with smokes like burning sulphur, was a common practice. And the rose was also considered to have other valuable medicinal properties.

Pliny the Elder, writing in AD 76, said that the rose could be used in the treatment of thirty-two conditions, including inflammation of the eyes, the ears and the mouth, stomach ache, toothache, insomnia, the healing of wounds, and for what he called 'purification of the mind'.

Certainly dried *Rosa gallica* var. *officinalis* was available in the stores of the apothecary in the medieval monastery. And in 1807 the rose growers of Provins in France (one of the many towns in the world, including Aberdeen in Scotland, which is called 'the town of the roses') obtained a government warrant that their unguents derived from roses would be used in all public and military hospitals.

While the long-held belief that products based upon roses could be aphrodisiac has been reluctantly abandoned, aromatherapists today still think that rose oil can be useful in treating frigidity. Meanwhile, Professor Dietrich Wabner in Germany has been working with rose oil for the treatment of the common cold and the herpes virus responsible for cold sores.

Medieval apothecaries are said to have dispensed infusions of rose leaves and petals, particularly those of the astringent *Rosa damascena*, as a palliative for coughs. An infusion of hips or milk in which rose petals, had been softened was used to soothe tired eyes. Damascena petals were often ingested in honey to control coughs.

In 1672, an early traveller to America, John Josselyn, reported that he had found a conserve of roses a useful cure for seasickness. Even if the benefits of some of these treatments are dubious, there is no doubt that rose hips, particularly those of *Rosa canina* – the common dog rose of our hedgerows – contain more vitamin C than any other fruit and are still used as a source of that vital product.

The rose has long been associated with health, as in this poster for the Bagnoles de L'Orne where the rich combined the pleasures of the thermal bath with the casino and tennis.

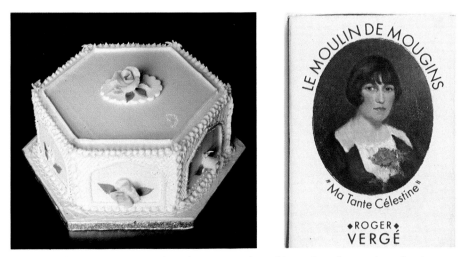

Left Apart from using rose petals and rose-water in making cakes, the rose has often been used as a symbol of love in cake decoration. This wedding cake was designed by William Robinson and made by Perrin Jessup.

Right The English rose may be a cliché, but the French also use a rose to symbolize all that is best in their womanhood, as on this matchbox given away at one of their greatest restaurants.

In the early years of World War II, citrus fruit from abroad was in very short supply and to make up for the deprivation of vitamin C children were dosed with a syrup made from rose hips. Many of them didn't like it because it had an unfamilar flavour. Children in the suburbs and country districts were taken out of school to collect the hips from the hedgerows. Although the escape from books was initially welcome, it was a very scratchy and often a bitterly cold activity which lost its popularity as fingers almost froze and then, infuriatingly, chilblains developed.

Rose hips simmered in water until they have fully softened, then mashed and left in a jelly bag to drip overnight, can make a nutritious jelly, when the liquid is mixed with sugar and lemon juice and boiled until it sets. But far more flavoursome is a jam made from the petals of fragrant roses from which the bitter inner ends have been detached. A speciality of the French town of Provins, its other ingredients are white sugar, honey and lemon juice.

Rose petals have for centuries been used in the kitchen in many other ways. After the Romans had brought the vine to northern Europe, the petals of the rose were used to improve the flavour of and impart some sweetness to the often inferior and rather acid wines which resulted from grapes grown in the north.

Rose petals with the bitter ends removed are still suggested as ingredients to give delicate flavour to sandwiches, salads and even

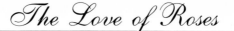

vinegar. Butter blocks coated with petals pressed into their surface and changed several times over two or three days will also adopt some of their fragrance and flavour. This can be captured more permanently when crystallizing the petals by boiling them in a sugar solution, when they are used for cake decoration. Petals for these culinary uses are usually collected on bright sunny mornings when the dew has gone from roses which are just opening fully. A few drops of the pure rosewater obtained when distilling rose petals can be used to provide a lightly scented flavouring for fruit or cream dishes. The dried leaves of *Rosa canina* are also said to make an infusion which some people prefer to tea.

Eating and drinking roses seem destined to remain a small-scale activity for the connoisseur. Not so smelling of roses, which might well become big business for Britain if Dr Wilde's process catches on. The British have a reputation for inventions which are then developed by other countries into large-scale businesses, but perhaps rose oil extraction may be the exception that proves that a cottage industry can become a national success.

XI

Rosa mutabilis

Apart from roses themselves, there are many other members of the family *Rosaceae* which are almost as widely known. They include such frequently encountered genera as *Crataegus* (the hawthorns) and *Malus* (the apples). And, to understand the ways in which scientists have been manipulating roses destined for our gardens, it is necessary to consider their work with other members of the family and also with many less closely related plants, which initially may offer more opportunity of investigating ways of altering plant forms, colours and other characteristics.

In July 1987, with a few deft flicks of their scalpels, Dr Brian Power and his colleagues in the plant genetics manipulation group of the Botany Department at Nottingham University cooked up something in their laboratory very noteworthy for all lovers of a good apple tart. They saved for posterity the admirable characteristics of that most outstanding member of the *Rosaceae* – the 'Bramley Seedling', using a micropropagation technique.

This method of asexually reproducing plants is of particular value to propagators working with families like roses because, although cross-fertilization between flowers is possible, it means that plants developing from seed never exactly resemble their parents. However, it took a long time for botanists to discover how to achieve micropropagation, which is a superior equivalent of cloning by striking cuttings.

Over a century ago botanists discovered that fragments of plant tissue could be kept alive for significant periods in nutrient solutions. But it was only in the 1960s that a Frenchman, Georges Morel, working with orchids, put together the ingredients necessary in a nutrient medium so that a few cells could be made to grow, multiply and then differentiate into roots and stems – and ultimately become plants which would grow independently in soil.

Apart from salts of the major elements and trace elements of which plants are composed, he also had to add the plant hormones which trigger both cell division and differentiation into different types of tissue. Morel worked with hybrid orchids which were beautiful but sterile. Following his lead, other botanists tried to multiply other plants in the same way and usually found that for each family they had to modify the growing medium slightly before it could be made to work. However, the rewards of perseverance

---

PREVIOUS PAGE

The first cultivated variety introduced by the breeder David Austin was this 'Constance Spry', a cross between the Gallica 'Belle Isis' and the Floribunda 'Dainty Maid'. It was named in 1961 in honour of the woman who founded the famous flower shop in London and dedicated much of her time to the pursuit of old roses.

Dr Brian Power of Nottingham University with a clone of the original Bramley apple tree, which can be seen in bloom behind.

were high because it enabled new hybrids to be multiplied for trial and sale much more quickly. Whereas potatoes only reproduce themselves about nine-fold in a single generation, a few cells can be turned into thousands of plants in a year in a laboratory. That is why micropropagation has become one of the genetic engineers' most valuable tools.

In practice, tiny portions of the rapidly growing tips of plants are dissected under a microscope in a sterile cabinet. They are initially grown in a nutrient fluid in vibrating glass flasks, before being transferred to nutrient jelly surfaces to differentiate into embryonic roots and stems which can be grown on to become normal plants.

The original Bramley tree which grew from a pip sown between 1809 and 1812 by young Mary Ann Brailsford in her family's garden at Southwell, Nottinghamshire, still exists and bears fruit every year. But because for nearly two centuries cuttings from it refused to form roots, and apples which are cross-pollinated do not breed true from seed, it has only been possible to reproduce it by grafting shoots onto rootstocks derived from crab apples. This is a process begun by a nurseryman called Merryweather who was impressed by the fruit he saw on the tree in 1876 after the property had been bought by a Matthew Bramley. Those first grafts developed into what Merryweather called 'Bramley's Seedlings', and all the Bramleys grown in gardens and orchards today are derived from them by repeating the grafting process.

Over the years, however, the shoots used in grafting may have subtly changed in character owing to natural mutations or because of being grown on alien roots. And today's stock of Bramleys sold by the nurseries may not have the capacity to withstand attacks of scab disease so well, resist virus infection so resolutely or produce apples with quite such a high vitamin content as those of the original trees. And since until recently the original tree was unique, there was no way of finding out why, because to carry out proper trials a large number of trees are necessary. But now, thanks to their success in growing whole plants from tiny sections of the tissue of the original tree, the Nottingham researchers will be able to make such trials possible in future.

This is a splendid example of the way in which scientists can manipulate plants to foster the aims of conservationists by preserving the characteristics of existing varieties. Brian Power, nevertheless, like generations of plant breeders and geneticists before him, admits that the technique which he employed will continue to serve the interests of breeders who are essentially 'in the business of altering plants or create totally new varieties, which is a process that has been going on for as long as man has been farming and gardening'.

The earliest husbandmen must obviously have relied solely on selection for improvement – choosing seed from the sturdiest and highest-yielding plants in one season to sow during the next. The same process is still used to 'improve' new plants discovered in the wild which seem worth developing for the garden – the aim usually being to produce more robust plants with larger or greater numbers of more brightly coloured flowers, appearing over a longer season. By pandering to man's insatiable desire for novelty, it is a procedure which many gardeners have criticized as mere vulgarity.

Nevertheless there is evidence that as early as the twentieth century BC, the Chinese were already at it and seeking even greater changes by hybridizing chrysanthemums. And although ignorant of the details of sexual reproduction in plants, they clearly understood that men could affect the outcome by ensuring contact between the flowers of different plants.

This is certainly something which was understood by the Assyrians in the seventh century BC: they have left relief carvings showing farmers using pollen to fertilize the flowers of palms. And they, like all subsequent breeders, must have realized that by cross-fertilization it was possible to produce plants which were in many respects unlike their parents, and must have eagerly imagined the outcome of the process.

Nearly two thousand years had to elapse before the age of real understanding dawned. In 1760 the Swedish botanist Linnaeus reported seeing pollen tubes emerging from the pollen of *Sprekelia formosissima* – a type of amaryllis. Then, in 1827, Adolphe Brongniart saw the process being completed when witnessing the pollen tubes of *Datura* enter the style; he correctly concluded that this must happen before the ovules could be fertilized and set seed.

In 1760 the Swedish botanist Linnaeus (real name Carl von Linné) pioneered research into plant breeding. Here he is dressed in Lapp costume before setting off on an expedition at the age of 25.

It took another century and a quarter before the fine details of the mechanics, mathematics and biochemistry of sexual reproduction in plants were finally revealed. In that time, improved microscopy has enabled botanists to observe the secrets of cell division and to understand that it is the division and recombination of the chromosomes on the nucleii of the pollen and ovule cells which determine how plants transmit characteristics to their offspring.

By determining the structure of the actual genetic material – the DNA of which chromosomes are composed – Watson and Crick in 1953 helped geneticists to predict which sections of chromosomes were responsible for particular characteristics. This understanding made them realize that they would be able to interfere with the normal mechanisms of heredity by adding or taking away portions of the DNA. But before that was easily possible, it was necessary to work on individual plant cells which had been denuded of their thick cell walls. Edward Cocking, Professor of Botany at Nottingham University, found a way of doing this in 1960 by digesting them away with enzymes to form what are known as protoplasts. They were initially produced to enable work on plant viruses to be carried out.

In 1970, Brian Power realized that, once naked, some protoplasts doubled in size by fusing with their neighbours; he and the

Nottingham team showed it to be a procedure that could be encouraged chemically and electrically, and that ultimately – thanks to micropropagation techniques – new plants could be grown from the fused protoplasts and multiplied rapidly in the laboratory.

It was also realized that the fusion of protoplasts might permit hybrids to be made between plants which are not interfertile in nature and between different species of the same family. That has now been shown to be frequently possible.

But fusing protoplasts has also permitted considerable success in making those crosses which are much rarer in nature, such as those between entirely different families of plants. This means that there are reasonable hopes that one of the holy grails of breeders – the true blue chrysanthemum – may become a reality, since it may be possible to produce crosses between chrysanthemums (which don't produce blue flowers) and asters (which do).

Meanwhile, by using advanced breeding techniques, such as introducing new genes to established plants, it has been possible to produce lettuce which are resistant to mildew – and these are now widely grown commercially.

To gardeners, one of the most interesting achievements of the genetic engineers of Nottingham has been the production of a much branched and genuinely trailing version of petunia. Although the flower bells are not yet considered colourful or large enough to make the plant commercially interesting, it is likely that, using the godlike powers which would have had them burnt at the stake in the Middle Ages, breeders using the techniques pioneered at Nottingham will shortly achieve a really interesting new petunia. It is also likely that in future breeders will be able to produce one of their long-term targets – a genuinely blue rose.

Meanwhile, over the past twenty years, breeders have been responsible for several interesting developments. One of the most remarkable resulted from crosses made by the Hertfordshire breeder, Jack Harkness, between roses and their nearest natural relative, *Huthemia persica* (sometimes called *Rosa persica*) which has single blooms with a red eye. The aim of Harkness's hybridization programme was to try to introduce the red eye characteristics into roses where it was previously unknown.

After many failures and with great persistence, Harkness ultimately succeeded with a 'Canary Bird' × *R. persica* cross called 'Tigris'. This canary-yellow single bloom with a red eye, introduced in 1985, is believed to be the first lovely hybrid of *R. persica* to be offered commercially. It was followed in 1986 by the reddish salmon with red eye 'Euphrates', and in 1989 by a *R. rugosa* × *R. persica* salmon-pink and red-eyed hybrid 'Nigel Hawthorne', and a

Rosa persica redrawn after Redouté by Krüssmann: it is found growing wild from Persia (Iran) to Afghanistan.

sulphur-yellow, crimson-eyed 'Canary Bird' cross called 'Xerxes'.

General bloom colour has also undergone marked changes. The rose vermilion 'Superstar' bred by Tantau in Germany, which appeared in 1960, introduced colours with an unusual (almost unnatural) brightness and intensity which have been described as 'electric' or even 'plasticy'.

Less garish have been the introduction of broken-coloured or 'hand-painted' roses, like the first of its type, 'Picasso', produced by the famous New Zealand-dwelling Ulsterman Sam McGredy, who began to market it in 1971.

The introduction of 'Silver Jubilee' by the Scottish breeder Alex Cocker in 1978 did a great deal to change breeders' views about the importance of a good foliage as a breeding objective. In the past, blooms seemed to dominate the breeders' objectives, but often the best blooms were borne on thinly garnished and straggly stems. With its robustly bushy characteristics and luxuriant shiny foliage, 'Silver Jubilee' demonstrated that roses could, like many other garden plants, look good even before they came into bloom or when flowering was over for the season.

Other aspects of habit have also preoccupied breeders latterly. Some of them have been concerned with meeting landscapers' requirements. In an era when labour is costly, demand has grown for low-maintenance weed-suppressing ground covers such as tough, shrubby and low-growing roses. Breeders like Reimer Kordes in Germany introduced the varieties 'Grouse' and 'Partridge' in 1984 to fill this rôle. And the charming 'Nozomi', bred by the Japanese amateur Toru Onodera, has also proved extremely popular with both municipal authorities and gardeners since it arrived in Britain in 1968.

The miniaturization of the rose, to enable it to be grown as an indoor pot plant, had already become a serious business early in the century, but more recently it is breeders like Pedro Dot in Spain and Ralph Moore in California who have greatly advanced the art. One of Moore's greatest triumphs was to introduce old-fashioned moss-type blooms to miniatures, like his 'Dresden Darling' which has been greatly admired since its introduction in 1975.

A less exaggerated reduction in the scale of roses has led to the development of compact 'patio' varieties, which are suitable for the much smaller town gardens common today; such roses can be grown very satisfactorily in planters or tubs.

Not all the developments mentioned above have been equally welcomed by nurserymen or gardeners. Sometimes opposition to them has been due to a common loathing of change. But often it has been hard not to sympathize with their reservations. During the 1960s and 1970s much of the breeders' efforts seemed to be devoted to striving for a waxy perfection of the Hybrid Tea bloom or remontant characteristics, with no regard for other aesthetic considerations such as the general appearance of the bush, the freer charm of the older, 'less worked' varieties or the capacity to fill the evening air with a delicious fragrance. Real rose lovers found these productions vulgar and offensive.

However, among the trade it is the introduction by some nurseries of rose plants derived from micropropagation which has caused the greatest controversy. In the past, the majority of commercially offered roses were grafted onto rootstocks like the wild *Rosa canina* – the common dog rose – for two principal reasons. Two-year-old *Rosa canina* roots usually have a very neat and regular shape which makes packing the grafted rose easy for the nurseryman. But, more importantly, many varieties of rose only express their full potential when grafted onto a vigorous wild rootstock, in preference to simple propagation by cuttings when new plants develop their own root systems. Many growers now claim that micropropagation results in roses always growing on their own roots, with the disadvantages of reduced vigour which that usually engenders.

Since this 'factory' technique of multiplying roses is almost inevitably going to become more and more widely adopted, following the success of the Nottingham researchers, it is possible that in future one of the breeders' objectives might have to be to develop hybrids which are particularly suitable for micropropagation. For their parent stock they are likely to use those species which are known to make good roots of their own and to perform outstandingly on them.

Undoubtedly, we are still only in the pioneering days of such advanced techniques as micropropagation. Although there will be problems in its adoption – just as, in its earliest days, grafting appeared to be a strange and unnatural technique – but there is little doubt that the development of the rose will benefit from the newest discoveries of the plant geneticists.

While rose breeding as a profession is undoubtedly growing

more specialized year by year, no ordinary gardener should die without once having tried to breed a rose of his very own. And it isn't difficult because most floribundas and hybrid teas will readily interbreed.

Buy two likely container-grown plants at the garden centre which are showing plenty of bud. Try a white and red in the hope that some of the progeny will have pink petals. They will have to be kept indoors so you must keep them well fed and watered.

Ripe pollen from the male parent is best obtained when the flower is fully open. Close examination with a hand-lens will reveal the pollen as a yellow powder thickly coating the anthers at the tips of the stamens. Remove the stamens entirely, using a pair of fine-pointed tweezers. They will then remain fresh for several days inside a small closed, transparent plastic box – provided they are kept cool and dry and free from contamination by tiny pieces of torn petal or other plant debris.

Then timing is the really crucial factor. The stigmas of the female parent must be receptive but they must be caught before they have been naturally pollinated. Do that by examining the

'Leverkusen', bred by Kordes and released in 1954, is a fine example of a vigorous modern climber which will flower from June through to October.

developing flower buds at eight o'clock each morning. Loosen the ones which are likely to begin opening that day (the fattest ones, already showing their petal colour). With tweezers strip the sepals, petals and stamens from each of these buds, leaving only the exposed central stigmas. Then dip the tip of a finger into the plastic box of stamens and sprinkle a light dusting of pollen over all the stigma heads. Then enclose each bud in a small paper bag, fitting like a loose mitten and fastened to the stem with twine.

The process of fertilization takes between five and seven days, and the bag should not be removed until the light-coloured disc around the stigmas has darkened.

Flower buds pollinated in this way will develop into normal hips, and the gardener has nothing further to do until they are fully ripe in November. The hips then should be gently broken open so that the pips – or more correctly, achenes – containing the seeds can be scooped out without damage. Each hip will contain anything from one to forty viable seeds capable of growing into plants of a new variety.

They are sown at ½ inch intervals, just below the surface of seed compost, in a plastic seed pan labelled with details of the parents. Kept just moist in a cool airy place, and protected from frost and mice, most of the seeds should have germinated by the end of February. In late March or early April, once they have developed two pairs of true leaves (and provided they have shown no obvious faults), they should be transferred to 3½ inch pots containing John Innes No. 2 compost. If kept in a glasshouse, the seedlings should form their first tiny flower buds when they are about 3 inch high.

Rosa principalis

XII

The flower which has been the image of love – spiritual and physical – and a favourite of poets, painters and musicians over the centuries – has also been a symbol of power. Not just Flower Power but specifically Rose Power, as is shown by the large number of rulers who have taken over the rose as a means of marking their majesty. For the poet Browning's Patriot, it was 'Roses, roses all the way!' We may, however, reasonably question whether rose buffs have not gone too far in claiming that the rose has meant power since the earliest of days.

A drachma from Rhodes; the reverse shows a fully opened rose surrounded by seeds.

Krüssmann concludes that the oldest coins with impressions of roses on them come from Rhodes as late as between 400 and 80 BC. Claims made for the rose motif go much further back. There are many early examples of rosettes (i.e. multi-petalled flowers) as artefacts or decorations found in places of power. Examples in Krüssmann's book are shown opposite and the famous 'rose' at Knossos is discussed fully in the chapter, Rosa picta. A model of the ancient city of Nineveh (now in the Louvre) has examples of rosettes, some six-petalled, which also might be roses. Even as late as the era of Herod in Christ's time, the rose which is said to have been his symbol of office is not, Krüssmann warns, illustrated in any of the archaeological literature.

We are on safer ground nearer to the present time. Both sons of Henry III (1207–72) used the rose as a badge. Prince Edward (later

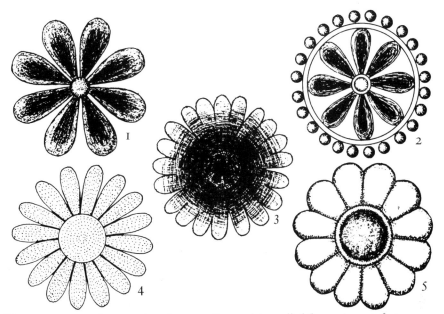

There are many early examples of rosettes (i.e. multi-petalled flowers) as artefacts or decorations found in places of power. Examples in Krüssmann's book are from the headband of a Hittite ruler (1), from a representation of a Sassanid king (2), from Hadrian's Arch (3), from the Palace of Nebuchadnezzar (4), from the ceremonial pedestal of King Tukultiminurtas (5), similar to others at Persepolis, and the famous 'rose' at Knossos.

Edward I) is said to have been the first King of England to wear a rose. He chose a golden one. Edward secured peace in the kingdom (his father was an ineffective ruler – by dispatching Simon de Montfort, head of the unruly barons, at the battle of Evesham in 1265. Following this he was able to leave the country on a crusade. Much is made – without any evidence – of the possibility that roses were brought back to England from the crusades.

More important for rose historians is the interest which Edward's brother Edmund Crouchback took in the rose. He was first Earl of Lancaster, and it is said that after an expedition to Provins in France, he brought home their red rose *R. gallica maxima*. Because there were no male Lancastrians, Blanche (the sole heiress) was made Duke of Lancaster. She married John of Gaunt in 1362, and their son became the first Lancastrian king, Henry IV. His descendant Henry VI fought what we now call the Wars of the Roses. At the time, they were called nothing of the sort.

It is true that the faction against which Henry VI waged war was headed by a man who also took a rose for his badge. It was a white rose and was probably an indigenous variety *R. x alba* (although it is found all over Europe and may have been brought to Britain by the Romans). The red roses in Britain at this time, perhaps indigenous, were *R. canina* and *R. rubiginosa*.

Henry VII (1457–1509) holds the rose that symbolized the fusion of the York and Lancaster families. The rose also figured prominently in his coinage and he undoubtedly believed that the symbol of the united roses would help him to retain the crown. The rose remains a symbol of the monarchy to this day.

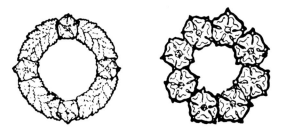

Rose chaplets such as this were worn by the nobility in the Middle Ages, either with just four blooms at equal intervals (left) or made up entirely of roses (right).

We do not know what roses – what species – were adopted by the Lancastrians – except that they were red. As noted above, Edmund is said to have adopted the *R. gallica maxima* after a visit to Provins in France. When he went there in 1279 the British controlled much of France. Edmund's mission was to avenge the murder of the English governor and suppress a rebellion by the local populace. The red rose was a symbol of Provins, but there is no evidence that when the conquering hero Edmund returned to England he adopted it as his badge as Duke of Lancaster.

Indeed, he may well have adopted the rose before he went to France, possibly at the same time as his step-brothers' mother also displayed a rose as her badge. Roses ran in the family, so to speak. Another 100 years were to pass before the House of York was founded: like the Lancastrians, it was an offshoot of the Plantagenet dynasty. Incidentally, the Plantagenets are said to be so-called because Geoffrey of Anjou, father of Henry II, wore a sprig of broom in his cap (*Planta genista*). The head of the house was Richard, Duke of York, and it is said to be his son, another Edward, who chose the white rose. The wars of succession, fought between the Houses of Lancaster and York, began in 1455 with the battle of St Albans.

Why, then, are they today called the Wars of the Roses? Two romantic writers are responsible. The first was William Shakespeare, who in one of his earliest plays, *King Henry the Sixth Part I*, has Richard Plantagenet (later Duke of York) urge his supporters, at a meeting in the Temple garden: 'From off this briar pluck a white rose with me.' The Earl of Warwick does so, but others, including the Earls of Somerset and Suffolk, prefer to 'pluck a red rose off this thorn', so supporting the Lancastrian party. A lot of talk (in blank verse) follows on the subject of white roses turning red when they are stained with blood, and Shakespeare does not miss an opportunity of referring to cankers and thorns.

Noted for his manipulation of historical facts, Sir Walter Scott decided to dignify these squabbles with the name Wars of the Roses.

The armour was made under the direction of Jakob Halder (1555–1607), master of the Royal Workshop at Greenwich, which was established by Henry VIII for his personal use and for the manufacture of presentation pieces of princely magnificence. The rose motifs alternate with fleurs-de-lis.

The quarrel between the Dukes of York and Lancaster, made much of in Shakespeare's plays, came to a head, according to legend, around the rose bushes growing in the garden of the Temple in London.

This was in his book *Anne of Geierstein or The Maiden of the Mist*, a somewhat laboured novel published in 1829, when Scott was writing as fast as he could to make money to repay a debt of honour. The name stuck and, coupled with Shakespeare's dramatic handling of the subject in three of his plays, the wars have since held a romantic place in the popular imagination.

There is further confusion about whether the York or Lancaster roses resulted in what is now 'the badge of England', the Tudor rose. As a heraldic device, the rose was already in common use – for example, the Lord Darcy had taken one as early as the thirteenth century, copying his design from the rose of the hedgerows with its five petals.

There is a third rose, according to Krüssmann, *R. damascena* 'Versicolor', called the York and Lancaster, which he assures us is not in fact a combination of the badges of the families. First described in 1551, Krüssmann says it is a sort of *R. damascena*, sometimes white, sometimes pink, and sometimes flecked with white and pink. It would be appropriate if this were the basis of the Tudor rose, rather than a 'combined' rose from the two houses,

The frontispiece to the 'Song of the Rose Garden' from the *Heldenbuch*, illustrates the Knights and their Ladies in the garden at Worms. The book is dated *c.*1500. The *Heldenbuch* shows two warriors being decorated with chaplets of roses before they set off to battle. The text says 'Here fought Dietlieb von Steyer and Walther von Wachsenstein. And each of them wore a chaplet of roses'.

since the wars had in fact no specific connexion with either Lancashire or Yorkshire – indeed for much of the period most of Yorkshire supported the House of Lancaster. The Tudor rose, in fact, was a design put together to commemorate the marriage of Elizabeth of York and Henry of Lancaster, the latter being the founder of the house of Tudor, Henry VII.

The power of the Church, as well as the power of the State, was sometimes embodied in the rose. It was the Pope's custom to bless a golden rose and send it to the ruler of a Catholic state as a token of esteem. With it went the following message.

> Accept this rose at our hand who, albeit unworthy, holds the place of God on earth, by which rose is typified the joy of the heavenly Jerusalem and of the Church Militant by which to all the faithful in Christ is manifested that most beauteous flower, which is the joy and crown of all saints. Recieve, then, thou dearly beloved son, who art, according to the age, noble, potent and endowed with many virtues, that thou mayest be more fully ennobled with every virtue in Christ our Lord, as a rose planted by the streams of many waters.

It was, nevertheless, kings and queens who made the most of rose power. As already noted, Edward I had his gold rose, 'stalked proper'. Elizabeth Tudor's Rose had the legend 'A rose without a thorn'. Queen Anne celebrated the amalgamation of England and Scotland by an emblem combining a rose and a thistle on one stem. (This is still on the colours of the 2nd Battalion Scots Guards.)

Heraldry – in the sense that it explains the meaning of such armorial bearings – came into general use in the Middle Ages. The consistent use of a specific image is not apparent in early European history. This is evident from the Bayeux tapestry, where in different parts of the fabric the same knight is shown with different devices on his armour or shield. It has been suggested that the Crusades brought about a greater sense of order and that by the twelfth century heraldry became a simple system for identifying those in a position of power. The idea spread like wildfire, and it was not long before the five-petalled rose was adopted by many of those who felt entitled to decorate themselves with a dignified device. The fashion began in France and Germany and spread to Britain.

The advantage of acquiring armorial bearings was that, from early days, it was recognized that a grant of arms conferred a grant of 'nobility' in the European sense or 'gentility' in the English. It was not long before corporate bodies (like guilds) and cities also felt themselves to be entitled to heraldic devices. The climax of heraldic activity in Britain was in the reigns of Edward II and Richard III, rather earlier than the Wars of the Roses. A revival occurred in the nineteenth century, much to the delight of Sir Walter Scott and other antiquarians, and continues to the present day.

Heraldry has over the years acquired its own language, one of which is that of 'common changes', amongst which are the rose and the demi-rose. The rose appears in several different forms. Most common is the rose with five petals and a boss of stamens, with the

On every Rose Sunday – the fourth in Lent – the Pope would give a vase containing a golden flowering rose (real gold, not paint) to the ruler who had made the most notable contribution to the Roman Catholic Church. This example can be seen in the Musée de Cluny, Paris, and was given by Pope Clement V to the Prince-Bishop of Basel in the early fourteenth century. It has been claimed that Mothering Sunday is a corruption of this ancient practice.

five sepal points showing between the petals. One variation has the sepals in a different colour to the petals, and this form is known as rose barbed. If the boss is coloured differently, that is rose seeded. The Tudor rose is double, red and white. The *Rose en Soleil* has the sun's rays extending beyond the petals. The rose slipped, surmounted by a crown, with a short stalk with two leaves attached, has become the Badge of England.

While the British monarchy has long hung on to the rose as its heraldic device and, by and large, has discouraged lesser mortals from using it, there have been no such restrictions elsewhere. In 1986, President Ronald Reagan signed Proclamation 5574, which officially recognized the rose as the national floral emblem of the United States. This was after extensive wrangling in Congress, with many congressmen lobbying for such rivals as the columbine and carnation.

The rose had already been adopted by some individual states. As early as 1916, Georgia claimed the 'White Cherokee' as its own, suggesting that it was indigenous to the soil. Thomas Christopher says that in fact botanists agree that it is Chinese in origin, having arrived in Europe from there in 1696. As another rose that gained official status under false pretences, Christopher cites that chosen by the District of Columbia, the nation's capital. This is the 'American Beauty' rose, adopted in 1925. Although claimed as a native, in fact it is French, the work of a breeder called Lédéchaux who put it on the market in 1875. It did not prosper in France and England, but flourished in America after it was introduced in 1886. New York also claims a rose as its emblem; the wild rose is claimed by Iowa, and the prairie rose by North Dakota.

In Britain, the Labour Party adopted a rose as its symbol in 1986, but this was not a case of lèse-majesté, nor did it have anything to do with the rose as a symbol of love or the brevity of life. It was chosen, according to Party records, because it was already the symbol of international socialism, having been the badge of virtually every such party in Europe since the turn of the

The 'Rose-en-Soleil' is a white rose, either single or double, in front of a sunburst. In its single form it was first used by Edward IV of England after his victory for the Yorkists at the battle of Mortimer's Cross; the double form is the Regimental Badge of the Grenadier Guards.

A ROYAL BIRTHDAY GALA

TO CELEBRATE
THE QUEEN MOTHER'S 90TH BIRTHDAY

IN THE GRACIOUS PRESENCE OF
HER MAJESTY QUEEN ELIZABETH
THE QUEEN MOTHER

HER MAJESTY THE QUEEN

HIS ROYAL HIGHNESS
THE DUKE OF EDINBURGH

AND
HER ROYAL HIGHNESS THE PRINCESS MARGARET
COUNTESS OF SNOWDON

*Stars from every part of the world of entertainment
come together in a glittering and unique tribute to this
greatly loved lady on the occasion of her 90th Birthday.*

All proceeds will be donated to service and allied charities

Among the Artistes appearing will be:
DAME PEGGY ASHCROFT • ROWAN ATKINSON
MICHAEL CAINE • PLACIDO DOMINGO
STEPHEN FRY • JAMES GALWAY
SIR JOHN GIELGUD • ROBERT HARDY
PATRICIA HODGE • DAME KIRI TE KANAWA
HOWARD KEEL • DAME VERA LYNN
WARREN MITCHELL • ROGER MOORE
ELAINE PAIGE • CLIFF RICHARD
THE ROYAL BALLET • WILLARD WHITE
(Further names to be announced)

Thursday 19th July 1990 at 8.00pm
LONDON PALLADIUM
Tickets £50 £75 £100 £150 £300
Applications together with remittance payable to 'London Palladium' (QM 90)
should be mailed to: ROYAL BIRTHDAY GALA,
LONDON PALLADIUM, ARGYLL ST., LONDON W1
and from usual Ticket Agents
Box Office: 071-437 7373 and 071-437 2055

The British royal family and the rose are inseparable – viz. this gala performance in aid of the Queen Mother.

century. The form in which the new British symbol was expressed owed little to other nations' socialists, however, and was the work of a commercial design agency working under the direction of the Party's Director of Communications, Peter Mandelson.

Money and power have always had close links, and financial power has inevitably played a part in the history of the rose. Never, fortunately, did the rose become the centre of financial speculation in the way that the Dutch tulip war or so-called 'tulip mania' led to the downfall of many investors in 1637. However, the distinguished garden historian Edward Hyams has explained that it was financial power which for many centuries ensured the survival of key types (or 'races' as he calls them) of the rose. He describes how, in the sixteenth century, 'great men's gardens were enriched with introductions other than the Centifolia derivatives.' These had come from southern Europe in the fifteenth century or earlier and their derivatives include the Cabbage roses, the Provence roses, the Moss roses, the Burgundy and the Pompon roses. The introduction was effected by religious orders.)

The gardens of the rich were then embellished with *Rosa* x *alba*, which in due course became the white rose of York, *R. gallica*, which arrived from South Europe before the end of the sixteenth century, as did *R. moschata* and the Persian yellow rose, *R. foetida*.

Left This caricature of Gertrude Jekyll is by her collaborator Edwin Lutyens.

Right Vita Sackville-West. Both ladies had a powerful influence on the choice of garden roses earlier this century.

As new varieties took their places in the grander homes, their predecessors were turned out and found their way into the gardens of the humbler cottages.

Hyams hypothesizes that a 'race' of roses like some of the old Centifolias would be passed on to a cottager, who, propagating them by cuttings, would expand the population by passing them on to neighbours and friends. Thus the cottage gardens became museums for 'old-fashioned' roses.

Sometimes the process of movement into the rich man's garden would be a swift one – such as followed the introduction in 1768 of *R. chinensis*, immensely popular 'because of its gene for almost perpetual flowering.' As one rose fashion followed another – with vogues for Hybrid Musks, Hybrid Perpetuals and so on – each was in turn relegated to the cottage garden.

It was always possible, therefore, for the sophisticated gardener to look to the cottage garden to find 'old-fashioned' roses no longer in vogue in his own grander gardens. Writers of influence, like Gertrude Jekyll or Vita Sackville-West, were able to bring about a reversion of the process amongst a much wider public so that the roses from the cottage were planted above their station, so to speak, across a wide social spectrum.

However there came a time when the cottager, and the small suburban gardener, could at last afford to buy his own roses, packaged cheaply by large multiple stores. 'The floribunda', says Hyams, 'has turned out to be, in a sense, the first 'race' of garden roses specifically for the cottager and small suburban gardener, who prefers it to the older roses . . . . It is very unlikely that sophisticated, rich gardeners will be able, ever again, to seek for 'old-fashioned' flowers in the gardens of working-class cottagers; however they may still find them in the cottage gardens of the retired middle-class gardener who has, perhaps, taken over the task of acting as museum curator'.

These 'museum curators' were spurred on in their turn by the efforts of the better gardening writers like Vita Sackville-West with

Modern middle-class 'cottagers' emulate the rose culture of their earlier and less affluent predecessors by growing roses. This fine example is a recent introduction 'Climbing Masquerade'.

her weekly *Observer* gardening column. She wrote, on 28 May 1950, a typical paean of praise for the old-fashioned rose. 'The roses are coming out and I hope everybody will take the opportunity of seeing as many of the old roses as possible. They may roughly be described as roses which should be grown as shrubs. . . .' She quotes an article from 'a serious journal' which said: 'In the twelfth century the dark red Gallic rose was cultivated by the Arabs in Spain with the tradition that it was brought from Persia in the seventh century'. Vita Sackville-West describes this as 'pure poetry' and her biographer tells us she admitted she was 'drunk on roses' by this time. But they had to be 'old' roses, not the dreaded Floribundas which she despised.

She sneered at 'conventionally-minded people [who] remark that they like a rose to be a rose, by which they apparently mean an overblown pink, scarlet or yellow object, desirable enough in itself, but lacking the subtlety to be found in some of the traditional roses'. She admits that these 'suffer from the serious drawbacks of flowering only once during a season, but what incomparable lavishness they give, while they are about it'.

So it was that the power of a woman, exercised this time through the written word, had its effect on the history of the rose, just as the power of a woman backed by Napoleon's wealth had made its mark a century and a half earlier.

Meanwhile the power of the rose continues to hold sway as a symbol of regional power, as was evidenced by a vigorous correspondence in the *Independent* newspaper during the early days of April 1990. The question had been asked, what flower should be worn by the British population at large on St George's Day? A Yorkshireman replied that he would be wearing a white rose, while others thought it should be red. Differences of opinion on the matter were epitomized in a letter from a Mrs Elwes of Somerset. Her view was as follows:

The English rose is not red (Lancashire, Labour) or white (Yorkshire) or a blend of the two (Tudor), but pink – the wild English hedge rose with its flat heraldic petals.

Rosa moderna

Rose breeding has been one of the most international of activities since man began to travel freely round the world. We have seen how he moved from country to country and continent to continent, seeking new species or hybrids to use in his cross-breeding programmes. But often gardeners would send cuttings of their own new varieties to breeders elsewhere. And the innocence of the activity and the pleasure which roses provided could even lead to closed frontiers being opened as when, for example, the Irish gardener who was making the famous rose garden for the Empress Joséphine at Malmaison was allowed to come to England to seek stock, at a time when relations between the two countries were greatly strained.

Francis Meilland revolutionized the commercial advantages of rose breeding.

This international interchange was fostered by the fact that one of the botanical characteristics of the rose makes it particularly amenable to travel. Given encouraging conditions, sections of semi-mature rose stems will strike roots, take as grafts or produce buds which can be grafted; provided pencil-sized pieces of rose stem are not allowed to dry out, they can be sent virtually anywhere and be capable of reproducing the characteristics of the parent plant when they arrive. The disadvantage of this convenient ability to travel was that quite soon after an interesting new hybrid had been created, perhaps after years of careful crossing work by a breeder,

PREVIOUS PAGE

David Austin named this shrub after his father Charles in 1973, by which time he had become established as a leading English breeder, famous for crossing 'old' roses with modern varieties to produce abundant flowers of an old-fashioned apprearance which are nevertheless repeat-flowering.

any rose grower could obtain a single cutting and within a few years be selling the rose in large quantities to gardeners, with no benefit to the breeder.

The best illustration of both the advantages and the disadvantages inherent in the ease with which the rose can be cloned is 'Peace', which is believed to be the most popular and best-loved rose ever bred. It was created by Francis Meilland, the famous French breeder, at his nursery near Lyons. The first cross which he made was between 'George Dickson' (a Hybrid Perpetual rose of unknown parentage which had been bred by A. Dickson of Ulster in 1912 and which, despite having rather weak stems, had very large, velvety, crimson double blooms which were highly fragrant) and 'Souvenir de Claudius Pernet' (which was bred near Lyons by Joseph Pernet-Ducher in 1926 to commemorate the death of one of his sons in battle in 1914. The result of a cross between 'Constance' and an unknown seedling, it had very large, thirty-petalled, double blooms of a pure yellow with darker centres, long pointed buds and fine glossy leaves).

Meilland crossed the result of that cross with another cross which he had made – between 'Joanna Hill' (a pale yellow, large double with a strong scent, which resulted from a cross made in 1928 between 'Madame Butterfly' and 'Miss Amelia Gude' by Joseph Hill of Richmond, Indiana) and 'Chas. P. Kilham'. The outcome of this cross was crossed with 'Margaret McGredy', a rose of unknown parentage raised by Samuel McGredy (III) at Portadown in Ulster. This genetic cocktail which has taken some 200 words to describe took several years to make. It involved painstakingly removing stamens from the flowers of the male parents, when the pollen was beginning to ripen, and using them to fertilize the stigmas of the female parents (which had had their stamens plucked away by hand). Seed from the resultant hips was planted to produce hundreds of seedlings, all of which were different and of which only a few would offer sufficient promise to be used in the next crossing programme. Initially, however, they all had to be planted in an orderly way so that their characteristics could be examined and meticulously recorded.

In such programmes, breeders are initially looking for attractive different blooms and good foliage. Anything which appears really promising is then grown on, to assess such factors as the size and shape of the mature plant, its general vigour and, most importantly, its resistance to pests and diseases. Only when the breeder is satisfied on all these counts does he consider multiplying it and introducing it to commerce. And most breeders say that as the result of making and testing several thousand seedlings, they

The famous rose 'Peace' which was the foundation of Francis Meilland's lasting fame.

would be unlikely to consider more than two or three suitable for commercial production.

Usually, while multiplying the commercial stock of a new variety by grafting cuttings or buds onto appropriate root stocks, breeders send samples of their new rose under a code name to be tested in comparative trials at one, or several, of the world's internationally recognized rose trial stations. They do this because a good performance in the trials can help to confirm their own belief in the outstanding qualities of their variety; if the performance leads to major awards, these greatly help to obtain publicity and create a market for a new variety.

One place where all European breeders wish to have their new varieties tested is the USA. And just prior to the war, in 1939, both developing air travel and five-day Atlantic crossings by fast ocean-going liners made this easy to arrange. Cuttings were sent to American rose growers who would graft them and arrange for the resultant plants to be included in the All America Trials.

To return to Francis Meilland, in 1939, when he realized that the rose which he had bred and selected under the code name 3–35–40 had outstanding qualities, Europe seemed poised on the brink of war. Histrionics developed into action when Hitler invaded Czechoslovakia. This prompted Meilland hurriedly to dispatch budding wood to collaborating growers in Germany and Italy, because he correctly anticipated that communication with his old friends there was likely to become difficult soon.

But even after the outbreak of war, as long as there remained in Lyons the consul from a still-neutral America, who greatly appreciated roses and who had become a frequent visitor to the Meilland nursery, there seemed no need for haste in sending budding wood across the Atlantic. However, this situation changed abruptly when in November 1939 the consul telephoned to say that he was being recalled and was due to fly to the USA the next day. While his baggage allowance was strictly limited, the consul said that he would be prepared to take a small 1 lb. parcel to America with him. It was thus that the first budding wood from rose 3–35–40 arrived in the hands of Pennsylvania rose grower, Robert Pyle, who, as he had done many times in the past for Meilland, propagated it and sent it on for trial in several regions of the USA.

Isolated initially in Vichy France under General Pétain and later under the full horror of Nazi German occupation, Meilland had no notion about how 3–35–40 was faring abroad. He was so pleased with its performance in continued trials in France, however, that in 1942 he decided to name it after his mother 'Madame A. Meilland' and introduce it to local commerce. Meanwhile, trials with 3–35–40 went ahead in Germany, Italy and the USA. As some recompense for nearly five years of misery and isolation, when the Lyons area was liberated Meilland discovered that he had become very famous among international rose breeders. In Italy, after outshining other new roses on trial, 3–35–40 was being sold under the name of 'Gioia' (Joy). Similar fine performances in German trials had led to its being offered as 'Gloria Dei' (The Glory of God). However, it was in the USA that 3–35–40 gained the greatest accolade. As the result of nationwide trials, it obtained the first prize and was given the highest rating ever achieved in the All American Rose Selection trials. And because this spectacular success was achieved in the year during which hostilities in Europe ceased, the American Rose Society bestowed upon 3–35–40 the additional honour of christening it 'Peace'. And that is the name under which it has since become known throughout the English-speaking world.

As the result of so much publicity, coupled with the fact that with its large high-centred delicately perfumed blooms of creamy yellow, pink-edged petals and beautiful deep green glossy foliage it is undeniably a most outstanding rose, more than an estimated 100 million plants of the variety have been sold world-wide since 1945. But the majority of those meteoric sales were made with no benefit to Meilland. Fortunately, one thing which he did gain from them was a greatly enhanced reputation as a rose breeder. This must have

On the left the rambler 'American Pillar' is, as the name implies, a rose which will virtually form a pillar of colour, as it does in the famous garden at Mandeston, Scotland. It was introduced by the American breeder Van Fleet in 1902.

given him the prestige necessary to accomplish what became thereafter his major mission in life – the establishment of international plant breeders' rights.

Meilland knew that, as early as 1930, breeders of new varieties of plants in the USA could patent them and earn royalties whenever they were propagated and sold, for a period of 17 years from their first registration. He was also aware that during the war Hitler also launched a royalty scheme, in an attempt to encourage less than enthusiastic Dutch cereal breeders to create more productive varieties to feed his armies. No such scheme, however, was available in the rest of the world to ensure that breeders were adequately rewarded.

Francis Meilland determined to change that anomaly: few people setting out to persuade the governments of many countries to introduce harmonized legislation to ensure plant breeders' rights could have been more strongly motivated. Sadly, his will was stronger than his body and after more than a decade of constant travelling and negotiation he died, in 1958, tragically young at only 46. Even as late as 1975, his wife Louisette, who carried on his rose breeding business, told the writer that she believed that it was the strain of so much work, in addition to running his nursery and breeding organization, that was responsible for his early death. However, she was happy that although Francis did not live to see plant breeders' rights framed in law, he certainly knew that the majority of the governments with whom he had been negotiating had agreed to introduce legislation.

In Britain, the relevant Act of Parliament was passed in 1964. That was even too late to protect 'Baccara', another Francis Meilland rose which he brought out in 1954 to augment further his international reputation as a breeder. With 'Peace' he had established himself as a master breeder of outdoor roses. The tight red buds of 'Baccara' soon became the favourite among long-stemmed greenhouse roses to convey thousands of messages of love about the world each day and demonstrated that as a breeder Meilland could also satisfy all the demanding requirements of the indoor growers. He would undoubtedly have been proud of the fact that 'Baccara' dominated the cut-bloom market until 1970, when the semi-double rosette-shaped pink-bloomed 'Sonia' emerged as the result of a hybridization programme conducted by his son Alain.

In the quarter of a century since plant breeders' rights were generally introduced a great deal of what Francis Meilland predicted has taken place. He knew that, given patent-type protection, growers would be encouraged to invest a great deal more time and money in highly scientific breeding programmes and that this would lead to more novelties being offered to gardeners. Many of these were to result from hybridization programmes directed by trained geneticists, backed by the latest in computer technology.

Meilland also realized that the new hybrids would be marketed in more aggressive and sophisticated ways, growing well-rooted into pots or offered for instant gardening at the garden centres (which were just beginning to play a significant role) or wrapped bare-root in fancy packs for sale on supermarket shelves.

Such a big-business approach towards rose production and sales inevitably meant that the trade has tended to concentrate in the hands of very large and highly capitalized organizations. Breeders, Meilland recognized, would have to expand quickly if they wished

to survive as independents. And apart from fighting for breeders' rights, which would give talented hybridizers the possibility of earning sufficient profits for survival, he set about creating an international business to exploit his own hybrids, which he called Universal Rose Selection. With offices in several countries, URS made marketing arrangements with prominent local breeders and propagators: maximum distribution and profit could be obtained from new varieties before other propagators had built up sufficient stocks to devalue them in the market, or before even more novel hybrids could replace them in the growers' catalogues.

Such highly evolved breeding and marketing arrangements did lead to a spate of new hybrids, to satisfy the growing demand from a public which has become increasingly interested in ornamental gardening as general prosperity and leisure time has increased.

This trend was first obvious in America where plant patents existed early and new approaches to marketing are often pioneered. In the early post-war years, the public preference was for fairly compact Hybrid Tea bush roses with a tendency to strongly pointed buds and rather rigid high-crowned blooms. These have tended to become less popular recently because many gardeners tired of their rather waxy allure, the gaudiness of some of their colours and the fact that many of them lacked fragrance. However, there is no doubt that some of the finest roses ever bred were produced in that period. And a feature of many of them was that they were far less prone to disease attacks and were more recurrent flowerers than many of their antecedents. By 1947, Eugene Boerner of Jackson and Perkins of Newark, New Jersey was marketing his splendid creamy-yellow 'Diamond Jubilee'. Meanwhile, 5000 miles to the south-west, Herbert Swim was working on splendid Hybrid Teas for the Armstrong Nursery in California. His deep gold 'Sutters Gold' was released in 1950, the apricot 'Mojave' in 1954, and the bright pink 'Royal Highness' in 1962.

Calling it 'Tropicana' in his native Germany, Mathias Tantau released in 1960 what became in the English-speaking world, the immensely popular 'Superstar'. With its vibrant light vermilion blooms it was one of the earliest roses to shock as well as please. Discriminating gardeners were inclined to shun its brashness but, realizing its great value in brightening up drab corners others bought it by the millions. Tantau's orange vermilion 'Duke of Windsor' was another fine Hybrid Tea released in 1969 which, despite the popularity of the man after whom it was named, failed to appeal as much to gardners as 'Superstar'. While a lasting reputation seems assured for Mathias Tantau as the man who bred 'Superstar', it may well be 'Fragrant Cloud' for which he will be best remembered. Introduced in 1963, this has coral-red very large flowers, shiny deep green foliage, vigorous growth and a particularly strong fragrance. It has such excellent characteristics that many breeders have chosen to use it as an influential parent in their own hybrids: Alec Cocker used it as a parent for 'Alec's Red' and Cants used it in producing their 'Just Joey'.

In 1967 the strong upright growth of the large-bloomed soft pink, double 'Blessings', from the great Nottingham breeder Walter Gregory, began to attract many gardeners. The appeal of 'Elizabeth Harkness', which the Hertfordshire breeder Jack Harkness brought out in 1969, was its unusual pastel-shaded creamy-buff blooms, which have pink to amber central marking to the petals. It was to have a more lasting attraction for gardeners than another fine Harkness release in 1972, 'Alexander', despite this tall hedging rose's similarity to the immensely popular 'Superstar'.

Apart from its huge bright crimson blooms, it was the resistance to disease and hardiness of Aberdeen breeder Alec Cocker's 'Alec's Red' which won it the most support when he launched it for gardeners in 1970. The unusual coppery orange 'Just Joey', released by Cants of Colchester in 1972, gained such a reputation for free flowering and strong fragrance that even in 1989 it was the top seller in that nursery's catalogue – and it looks like remaining a firm favourite with gardeners for years to come. The extremely successful German hybridizer Reimer Kordes produced, in 1978, the very large deep pink bloomed 'Sylvia', sold in the English-speaking world as 'Congratulations', which is one of the more recent notable Hybrid Teas.

Subsequently, while the search for good Hybrid Teas has continued, the emphasis on breeding programmes has shifted towards other forms of rose. The production of better Floribunda types has been one of the great preoccupations of breeders over recent years. These are the roses in which the blooms are clustered like a bouquet rather than presented singly like an emblem. It is a characteristic shared to varying degrees by the simpler species roses *Rosa multiflora*, *Rosa chinensis* and *Rosa moschata*. And apart from the charm of roses with that type of inflorescence, the best of them tend to flower for a long period and seem to offer gardeners better value.

One of the best of the early Floribundas, the pure soft pink double 'Queen Elizabeth', bred by Dr Lammerts in California, was launched in 1954 and had such strong and long stems that it soon became popular for tall rose hedges, or for setting in circles to form features like plant temples. Although still available, it has lost in popularity because it tends to become rather leggy unless carefully managed and pruned to shape.

'Bobby James', a very vigorous rose of the type which Peter Beales calls 'a scrambler', was released by Sunningdale Nurseries in 1961. Although its parentage is unknown, Beales believes it owes something to *Rosa multiflora*.

Though there have been plenty of attempts, no breeder can claim to have outdone Reimer Kordes in the production of a sparkling white floribunda since he produced his 'Iceberg' in 1958. To many gardeners it remains the perfect rose with both a lovely form and an astonishing fragrance.

Dark pink veins, clearly visible, permeate the lighter pink flesh of the cup-forming petals of 'Pink Parfait' which Herbert Swim bred for the Armstrong Nurseries in California in 1960. And they helped it to gain many prizes. The soft lilac-lavender petals of 'Ripples', bred by E.B. Le Grice at North Walsham in Norfolk in 1971, made it one of the most outstanding of the new generation. Floribundas. It was a similarly unusual yellow-amber hue which gained considerable popularity for Alec Cocker's 'Glenfiddich' after it was released in 1976. Appropriately, orange to almost tomato-red petals rather loosely arranged gave a strange and attractive allure to Northern Ireland breeder Pat Dickson's 'Beautiful Britain' when it was released in 1983. And its informality hinted at a growing predilection for less formal types.

Four really excellent climbing roses have emerged since the mid-1960s, though one of them – a climbing sport of 'Iceberg' which Cant picked up in 1968 – can hardly be said to have resulted from a deliberate breeding programme. 'Schoolgirl', released by

Sam McGredy in 1964, has orangey yellow petals which fade to an almost salmon pink and offered something rather different as a climber, with much of the carefree insouciance of its namesake. However, it has never quite had the appeal of Walter Gregory's 1965 gem 'Pink Perpétue'. With its recurrent rich carmine-pink blooms it has become one of the most frequently mispronounced and often-planted climbers of the modern era. Jack Harkness has always aspired to combine the formality of a perfect Hybrid Tea rose with the unruly, rather ragamuffin characteristics of a bold climber: he succeeded in doing it triumphantly with his large-flowered apricot and salmon 'Compassion', released in 1973.

As has been mentioned elsewhere, over the last two decades breeders have paid much attention to the need to provide much more compact roses suitable for growing in confined spaces, such as patios or raised beds. A perfect example of this type of rose is 'Penelope Keith' which was released in 1983 by Sam McGredy in New Zealand. It has well-formed, high-centred flowers of golden yellow petals which are darker on the undersides so that the blooms seem to smile more strongly as they open to meet the sun. With attractive light green leaves and an upright compact shape, this cultivar looks well even when not in bloom and merits place in every garden.

It is ironic that, with the exception of the miniature and compact roses, it is the very large shrub roses which seem to have had the most appeal to gardeners in an era when informality and 'the natural look' are most prized. Initially this led to a resurgence in the popularity of some fine early shrub roses, including 'Roserai de l'Hay', a seedling of unknown parentage selected by Cochet-Cochet in France in 1901, with dishevelled wine red blooms; 'Pink Grootendorst' with delightful frilly, clear pink petals, a sport from 'F. J. Grootendorst' selected by Grootendorst of Boskoop, Holland, in 1923 – all with *Rosa rugosa* genes; the bright scarlet single-flowered, arching-stemmed, 'Geranium', a *Rosa moyesii* seedling discovered at the RHS in 1938; Pedro Dot's *R. moyesii* hybrid of 1927 'Nevada' with its superb creamy flowers with prominent chocolate-brown stamens; and Wilhelm Kordes's delicate primrose-yellow 1937 hybrid of the Scottish *Rosa pimpinellifolia* 'Frühlings-gold'. Many gardeners discovered that the old shrub roses made splendid hedges because most of them have sharp thorns and make dense bushes. Some exceptionally fine hips in the autumn are another reason for their popularity.

It was the appearance of some of the fine old Bourbon roses and shrub roses like those mentioned above which first entranced David Austin, attracted him to hybridizing and ultimately led him

'Pink Perpétue' has become one of the most commonly grown climbers since it was introduced in 1965. Its name is commonly mispronounced, the correct version being 'Per-*pet*-u'.

to hold a unique place among modern rose breeders. Like many farmers' sons, his family anticipated that David Austin would ultimately take over running the family farm. Meanwhile, as a young man he was expected to learn the business by acting as an assistant to his father Charles. And there was certainly plenty to learn because Austin senior had acquired a fine reputation as a breeder of Hereford beef cattle which he fattened on his traditionally fruitful West Midland pastures at Albrighton in Shropshire. Initially all went well, as David under his father's patient tutelage absorbed an understanding of crop and animal husbandry. It was, however, his strongly developed aesthetic sense which began to create friction. In the early 1950s he started to become familiar and fall in love with old shrub roses.

This comparatively mild vice ought not to have raised problems if David had not become so seduced by the fragrance, the gorgeous colour palette and the bountifully free form of the ancient hybrids. To someone who had seen how the important characteristics of cattle could be blended by scientific breeding, the possibility of deliberately creating new beauties by cross-breeding old shrub roses with some of the more modern varieties seemed irresistibly tempting. After consulting old hands like gardening guru Graham Stuart Thomas, whose knowledge of shrub roses was unparalleled, David Austin began making hybrids himself.

An impatient curiosity is something which seems common to all breeders. And it is understandable that having made a cross they are anxious to witness the outcome. However, if many crosses have been made, that anxiety can seem to outsiders like a mania. To David Austin's father, realizing how preoccupied his son was becoming, it seemed like a damaging obsession. Serious farmers' sons, he argued, would devote that time, thought and energy to important farming concerns, not dissipate it messing about with roses. Charles Austin's experience as a husbandman had taught him that livestock farming is virtually a 24 hour per day job; that there is never really time to relax. Constant observation and vigilance is necessary because it is only by obtaining total familiarity with every beast in a herd that abnormalities which require attention will be noted. Animals cannot talk, but a real stockman can learn a lot from the hang of a head or the way a hoof is poised on the ground.

In retrospect David Austin says that he can understand his father's despair. But all gardeners must be grateful that he braved parental wrath because, by his hybridizing activities, he has brought into being a whole new race of what he calls English Roses – and made as significant a contribution to the breeding of garden plants as anyone else in the twentieth century.

The *Rosa pimpinellifolia* 'Frühlingsgold', bred by the famous Wilhelm Kordes in 1937, is still very popular. It flowers abundantly like this in mid-summer and may well bloom again later.

David Austin says that his main objective was to combine 'the form, character and growth of the Old Roses with the repeat-flowering habit and wider colour range of Modern Roses'. 'English Roses are, in fact, repeat-flowering Old Roses and may be said to carry on where the Bourbon Roses left off.' In his fascinating book, *The Heritage of the Rose*, David Austin provides a revealing account of his main breeding objectives and defines what one of his English Roses should be. It should have a natural shrubby growth with flowers which echo the forms of the Old Roses, i.e. it should have deep or shallow cups, rosettes, semi-double or single or any combination of these forms. It should have a strong fragrance, and colours should tend towards the pastel shades, though there are some deep pinks, crimsons, purples and rich yellows. Above all its appearance must be delicate and given good conditions it must repeat-flower well.

The steps which he followed to achieve these objectives were long and complicated, but he had his first real success when crossing E.B. Le Grice's 'Dainty Maid', a shell-pink Floribunda, with Parmentier's 1845 small, pale pink Gallica 'Belle Isis', to produce the hugely successful, very large pink-flowered 'Constance Spry' in 1961. It had many of the qualities which he was seeking but it was not repeat-flowering. To introduce this latter characteristic to his

A sweeping bed of 'Nevada', possibly a *Rosa moyesii* hybrid, bred by Pedro Dot of Spain in 1927.

genetic pool, Austin crossed 'Constance Spry' back to several modern hybrids such as 'Ma Perkins' (Jackson and Perkins 1952) and 'Monique' (Paolino 1949). Both these hybrids have a great capacity for recurrent flowering, which is something which most of the Old Roses lacked. The result of this crossing programme was a valuable pink line. A similar series of crosses led to a useful red line which gave Austin the basis from which to begin producing his English Rose breed. 'Golden Wings' (Shepherd/Bosley 1956) and 'Chinatown' (N.D. Poulsen 1963) were later introduced to bring with them their yellow pigmentation.

The success of 'Constance Spry' ultimately convinced Charles Austin that breeding and propagating roses might be a reasonable alternative way of using at least part of the family farm land and reconciled him to the fact that David had become an internationally-recognized rose breeder. David in his turn realized that nothing will keep land in better heart, no matter what you want to grow on it, than a decent herd of grazing beasts, which act as walking dung carts in the summer and create tons of wonderful farmyard manure when they are yarded on straw in the winter. So while rose

Amateurs have always played an important rôle in rose breeding and Albert Norman – one of the most notable twentieth-century amateurs – produced this beautiful floribunda 'Frensham' in 1946. It is seen here at Howick Hall.

production is now the dominant activity at Albrighton the cattle are never neglected. The rapprochement between father and son was joyfully commemorated with the release in 1973 of 'Charles Austin' a fine upright shrub with shiny leaves and very large cupped apricot-yellow flowers tinged with pink as they age.

While all Austin's early hybrids were well received, it was not until 1983 that his output astonished virtually every rose grower who saw them. In that year he launched three remarkable roses. Perhaps the most enchanting was the modestly charming 'Mary Rose'. It has loosely cupped strong rose-pink petals and a very strong bushy habit. The name was chosen to commemorate the recovery of Henry VIII's flagship from the Solent after more than 400 years beneath the water. 'Perdita' is considered by Austin himself to be the ideal small shrub with bushy, slightly arching growth to some 3½ ft. The fully double flowers are of medium size and their delicate apricot-blush coloured petals are arranged in shallow cupped formation. The tea scent of this rose is very strong, and it was awarded a Royal National Rose Society medal for fragrance in 1984. 'Graham Thomas', which Austin still considers one of the best roses that he has bred, completes the trio and is arguably the finest yellow rose for gardeners with enough space to allow its shrub rose characteristics their full expression.

After these triumphs, which made Austin's name echo round the rose world, it was interesting to see that only a year later he could demonstrate his great versatility as a breeder by bringing out 'Windrush', a delightful, innocent-looking, nearly single rose with a refreshing Scottish brier scent and a five-inch spread of pale lemon petals surrounding a boss of pale yellow stamens. Since then, in most years, he has seemed to be able to launch something new and exciting; keen rosarians always rush first to his stand at the Chelsea Flower Show in May to admire his latest novelty. It would be an exaggeration to say that the work of David Austin and others who have concentrated on breeding 'old' roses has swept the field. Commercially, there is still an immense sale for the Floribunda, despite criticism of garish colours and lack of scent in many varieties. However, we find writers like Robin Lane Fox stating authoritatively that 'It is a commonplace that modern bush roses are never so good as the old ones'. It is thanks to Austin's imaginative breeding that the rose is destined for a revival, even amongst those who feared that commercial developments of the new had destroyed the charm of the 'old' for ever.

Acknowledgements

T. E. Brown, the Manxman who wrote that awful but immortal line 'A garden is a lovesome thing, God wot', has as his next line the two simple words 'Rose plot'. It has sometimes seemed to us as we tried to unravel the story that there was indeed a plot to confuse, if not to mislead, the searcher after truth. So many definitive statements made about the rose have proved either to contradict other equally definitive assertions or to be uncheckable. Thus, many questions remain unanswered by us.

Our quest has inevitably caused us to be indebted to a wide range of friends and acquaintances who have made suggestions, lent us reference books and guided us in unknown fields. They have included Julian Shuckburgh, who originally conceived the idea of such a book, Jenifer Wates, William Husselby, Ginnie and Erin Lawlor, Dr Miriam Griffith, Dirk Kinnane, Dr Frances Clegg, David Austin, John Scarman, Peter Beales, Jack Harkness, Dr Peter Wilde, Alain Meilland, Reginald Fair, Dr Brian Power and, of course, our eminent sponsor, David Squire.

There does not seem to have been a general book on the rose since Peter Coates's *The Rose* (Weidenfeld, 1962), and we acknowledge with gratitude the ideas which it provoked. A major reference book for any study such as ours is the English translation of Gerd Krüssmann's *Roses* (Batsford, 1982), as is Peter Beales's *Classic Roses* (Collins, Harvill, 1985) and David Austin's *The Heritage of the Rose* (Antique Collectors' Club, 1988). Also essential reading are Graham Stuart Thomas's *Climbing Roses Old and New* (Dent, 1978) and *The Old Shrub Roses* (Dent, 1979). A recent book from America, *In Search of Lost Roses* by Thomas Christopher (Summit Books, 1989), has also been a source of inspiration, and we are glad to have been able to make reference to his engaging researches.

As regards specialist books, John House's *Renoir* (Arts Council, 1985) was a great help in the passages on that artist, and amongst other art books consulted was Wilfred Blunt's authoritative *The Art of Botanical Illustration* (Collins, 1951).

We have digressed from our purpose of thanking our sources, and those who helped us find them, such as the librarians of the Royal Horticultural Society, the British Library, the Bodleian Library, Oxford, the Warburg Institute, the Oxford City Library, the Oxford University Classics Faculty library, the library of the Royal Borough of Kensington and Chelsea, and Bernadette G. Callery of the New York Botanical Garden. Finally, we thank Angie Hipkin and Lizzie Boyd for their efforts in converting the manuscript into print.

Picture acknowledgements are as follows (reference is to page numbers): The Mansell Collection: 156; Josh Westrich: 7, 21, 39, 53, 71, 87, 107, 125, 149, 167, 179, 189, 203; Kenneth Scowen: 37; Vincent Page: 206; Peter Beales: 25 (left); John Scarman: 25 (right); Jack Harkness: 73 (left); Reginald Fair: 73 (top, and lower left); Graham Rose: 177 (left); Dr Brian Power: 181; M. Alain Meilland: 204; Gerd Krüssmann: 14, 24, 28, 41, 61, 96, 111, 130, 150, 165, 169, 174, 185, 190, 191, 193, 196, 198; Andrew Lawson: 23, 26, 29, 35, 83, 85, 173, 214, 215, 217, 218; Hugh Palmer: 13, 30, 34, 75, 76, 79, 80, 81, 187, 201, 208, 212, 219; The Bridgeman Art Library: 43 (Louvre, Paris), 56 (Christie's), 91 (Uffizi, Florence), 92 (St Martin's, Colmar), 95 (Château Malmaison), 103 (Courtauld Institute), 104 (Louvre, Paris), 109 (National Gallery, London), 112 (British Library), 116 (Alte Pinakothek, Munich) 117 (Prado, Madrid), 120 (Walker Gallery, Liverpool), 121 (Birmingham City Museums and Art Gallery), 127 (Wallraf-Richartz Museum, Cologne), 128 (Victoria & Albert Museum), 135 (Wallace Collection), 137 (Louvre, Paris), 138 (Christie's), 139 (Château de Compiègne), 146 (Musée d'Orsay, Paris), 158 (British Library), 192 (National Portrait Gallery, London); Sotheby's: 44, 48, 49, 50, 51; Victoria & Albert Museum: 27, 133, 143; Rosalind Mann: 105; Laporte plc: 60.

David Squire wishes to express his gratitude to the following: Eric Smith, last in line of the Smith family of rose growers established in the early part of this century; Jim and Pat Phillips, who have been involved in rose cultivation all their lives and have been instrumental in producing many new varieties from sports; James Mitcheson, whose expertise with the camera on special floral subjects has been outstanding, with the Violet Squire rose as an example; and Stella Munford, who has given so much help with typing and the secretarial side of this book.

$\mathcal{I}ndex$

SUBJECT INDEX

Illustrations are denoted by page numbers in italics

ROSE NAME INDEX

Illustrations are denoted by page numbers in italics